TALES
of a BEAR
HUNTER

TALES
of a BEAR HUNTER

DALE THACKER

Botetourt Nace Press
Troutville, Virginia

Copyright © 2025 Dale Thacker

All rights reserved. This book, or any portion thereof, may not be reproduced or used in any manner whatsoever without the express written permission of the publisher, except for the use of brief quotations in a book review.

Printed in the United States of America
First Printing, 2025
ISBN-13 (Trade Paperback): 979-8-9923495-0-4
ISBN-13 (eBook): 979-8-9923495-1-1

Botetourt Nace Press
dalethacker.com

Dedication

This book is dedicated to my granddad.

As a child, I loved going over to my granddad's to spend time with him and my aunt, Myrtle Conner. I loved helping him on his small, eighty-acre dairy farm. My granddad was a large, rough, and tough man. He stood six feet, two inches tall and weighed over three hundred pounds. My favorite pastime was sitting on my granddad's lap, or beside him, while he told me tales of bear hunting. These were the stories that helped make me into the bear hunter I am today.

Ernest Vaten Conner
March 8, 1886 to April 18, 1982
Daniel Boone was my childhood hero,
and my granddad was my real-life Daniel Boone.

TALES
of a BEAR
HUNTER

CHAPTER 1
Granddad

My granddad was a burly man, but he had a soft spot for his children and grandchildren. Ernest Vaten Conner got married at an early age to his childhood sweetheart, Clarice Cecily Holland. Like him, she was born and raised in Floyd, Virginia, and she was the love of his life. Shortly after getting married, they bought an eighty-acre farm in Botetourt County.

I don't remember a lot about my grandmother, but I remember that she was always lying on the living room couch. She was very ill—I believe she had had a stroke. Someone had to feed her, wash her, and help her use the bathroom. She died when I was ten years old. I wish I could have had more time with her when she was healthy. My grandmother had Monacan Indian blood; her grandmother was full-blooded Monacan Indian. My mom told me that Grandma used Native American healing methods she had learned from her parents.

My grandparents had eight children: two sons and six daughters. The first born, Ernestine Conner, died from whooping cough at just eleven months and eleven days old. Of all the family members, my Aunt Myrtle is the only one living now. She told everyone she was the smartest of the bunch because she never got married. To the best of my knowledge, she never even had a boyfriend.

Once I was old enough to help Granddad on the farm, I spent most weekends and some evenings after school there, planting and harvesting vegetables in the garden. I helped weed the garden, too, which was not my favorite chore, but I also took care of the chickens and fed the geese. We had quite a few chickens at the time that provided us eggs and meat. The geese I never liked because one of them pinched me when I was younger. Dang, did that hurt. They had chased me to the gravel pile, which I climbed onto, then screamed at the top of my lungs. Fortunately, my mom came to my rescue.

Over the years, we had some rather cool pets on the farm, such as raccoons. We also had groundhogs, which actually make very good pets. If you get them when they are young, they tame easily. My aunt had over thirty cats that I would help feed and water. At night, we'd put them in a large cathouse outside to prevent foxes from devouring them as snacks. But my favorite pets were two crows that lived in a large bird cage on the closed-in back porch. One of the crows had learned to mimic words and sounds, so whenever my granddad cleared his throat, the crow would follow suit, imitating the sound perfectly.

As I got older, I was given more jobs and responsibilities on the farm, such as milking the cows. This was so much fun, except when the cow suddenly felt the need to go to the bathroom. I had to grab the bucket and turn sideways to protect the milk, but the pee or poo would still always splash on me. Sometimes, the cats would sit there waiting for me to turn the udder toward them. Then, they would catch the milk midstream before it hit the ground. For them, warm, fresh milk was a delicacy.

I also started loading the old-fashioned, square hay bales onto the trailer to take to the barn, where I would stack them. I was a thin and lanky kid, so lifting that hay was extremely hard work. But boy, did that help build muscle.

One of my cousins, Ernest Guilliams, also lived on the farm. He was older than me, and both he and my granddad would teach me new skills. Now that I was a little older, I was learning to drive the old Ford farm tractor. I was also learning how to mow the fields and rake and bale the hay, which was a lot more fun than picking up all those hay bales later. But after some time, my granddad wasn't getting around as well as he once was, so he took to driving the tractor while Ernest and I found ourselves once again hoisting those hay bales onto the trailer.

My favorite time of day was evening, when all the chores were done. After supper, I would sit either on my granddad's lap or beside him as he told me stories. I had lots of cousins who would gather round, too. Granddad considered himself to be a bear hunter and never cared about other types of hunting, and of all the stories he told, those were the ones I loved the most. After you hear my favorite story of his, you will know why I considered Granddad to be my real-life Daniel Boone.

Granddad was out working in the fields one day, when from up in the holler, his bear hounds started bawling. Although he had others, Granddad's favorite hunting dogs were Bluetick Coonhounds. He said it was because he loved the sound of a Bluetick and because it had a colder nose than the other hounds. Anyway, he forgot all about the work he was doing and stood there, listening to his hounds. He knew they had the scent of a bear. But since it was just an occasional bawl, he knew it was a cold track, meaning the scent was old and harder for the dogs to detect.

As the track warmed up, though, the dogs barked faster and quickened their pace. They were about a mile up the holler now, moving from left to right, and from their barking, Granddad knew they probably had the bear in sight. They moved another half mile up the holler and stopped, still barking like crazy. The hounds had done their job: the bear was treed, meaning it had climbed a tree and the dogs were pawing at the trunk, barking furiously to keep the bear from coming down.

Granddad walked up the holler to find a nice-sized bear, weighing over three hundred pounds, sitting about fifty feet up a white oak tree, in a notch where a branch came off the main trunk. The dogs sat on their haunches, looking up into the tree and barking with every breath. They were jumping in the air, practically doing flips.

Normally, this is when my granddad would have shot the bear in the tree, but since he'd been working on the farm, he didn't have his gun. Instead, he looked around for a large stick to use as a weapon. He smacked the first couple of sticks he found against a tree, but they broke. He looked up. The bear was no longer in the notch but was now hugging the trunk. From experience, he knew the bear was seconds from sliding down the tree.

Frantic, he kept searching for a stick. At last, he found one and slammed it against the tree. *Thud.* It didn't break. With the perfect stick, my granddad was ready for battle.

He raised his stick as the bear slid down the tree. When it landed, he swung the stick harder than Babe Ruth would have swung a baseball bat. He hit the bear square in the head, but that only stunned it a little. Just before he swung again, the dogs swarmed the bear, and he had to be extra careful so he wouldn't accidentally kill one of his dogs. After a few more swings, the bear was dead.

He called his dogs off, and they started the trek down out of the mountains. When they got home, Granddad tied up his dogs and got someone to help drag the bear back so he could skin and butcher it. Bear meat, by the way, is delicious. I'm here to say it's my favorite meat. If you've ever tried bear meat and didn't like it, then it just wasn't prepared correctly.

My granddad loved his hounds and took good care of them. He had a unique way of making doghouses for them: Behind my granddad's house was a steep hill that he would dig holes into. Then he would place a fifty-five–gallon drum with one end open into each hole and fill dirt around it. This helped the dogs stay warm and dry in the winter and cool in the summer. He had about twenty of these doghouses. At times, he would let his dogs loose to run around the farm, but mostly he would keep the hounds chained up to prevent them from running out to hunt.

About twenty years ago, my Aunt Myrtle decided to trade the farm to a neighbor. She wasn't able to take care of the place the way she could before, and she had also been spooked by a series of flue fires. These days, she is living in a much more modern home on about four acres of land, so it was a good trade for both my aunt and the neighbor, who got some excellent real estate. I miss that farm a lot. The last time I visited, there were still remnants of the doghouses.

My granddad belonged to a large hunt club, a well-respected organization that always kept about a hundred members. They had a cabin located in the Glasgow/Snowden area of Rockbridge County, Virginia, the next county to the north of Botetourt.

Nowadays, I can't imagine hunting the way my granddad did, without the aid of modern technology, but his was the truest form of bear hunting. Back then, when hunting season came in, each member had a spot on the mountain to be at before daybreak. Typically, these spots would be on top of the highest peaks because it was much easier to hear, but other hunters would be stationed on the knobs of the "finger ridges" that came down off the top of the mountain.

The hunters had this down to a science. Typically, each hunter had two to four dogs. When one of the dogs got a "strike"—meaning they smelled a bear and started barking—the hunters knew which direction the bear would go once they cut their dogs loose. When those dogs got close to the other hunters, who were listening from their posts, they would cut their own dogs loose. It wasn't uncommon for twenty or more dogs to run past some of the hunters in pursuit of a bear.

Bears would usually bed down on finger ridges with thick pine, mountain laurel, and mountain ivy, so if none of the hunters had a track by the time everyone was at his post, the others would start down these ridges until they got a strike. Meanwhile, the other hunters would stay at their posts, ready to cut their dogs loose once the chase was on. They would listen closely to see when the bear became treed. Once the bear was treed, only the hunters nearest the tree would actually kill the bear. The other hunters would stay put, even after the bear was dead, knowing another track could get started.

I can't begin to imagine hunting this way today. Even a lot of old-timers out there don't know how to hunt like this. But it's worth knowing how to do it because even with all the technology we have today to track our hounds, laws could be passed in the future that restrict or prohibit its use, so it doesn't hurt to be familiar with the old-school methods.

As a child, I loved sneaking into Granddad's closet and taking down his cow horn. That's what he used to call his dogs back at night when the hunt was over. I had fun pretending I was calling the dogs. I would love to have that horn today, but I have no idea where it is. The contents of the old farmhouse were auctioned off. I'm sure that horn doesn't have the same meaning to whoever owns it now.

But I would cherish that old horn, and I would pass it down to my precious twelve-year-old grandson, Landon Gutshall. I took him bear hunting for the first time recently, and he loved it. Right now, he is learning to use a GPS tracking box, and by next year, he'll be better at it than me. The love of bear hunting seems to be skipping generations, though. My dad didn't bear hunt, and Landon's dad went with me a few times but didn't care much for it.

Here's another favorite story of my granddad's: On one hunt, he had hit upon a cold trail, and his dogs were giving out a slow bawl. It wasn't long until the dogs were heating up the trail and about ten of them were chasing the bear. Because of the intensity of the barking and how slowly they were moving, my granddad could tell they were walking the bear, a situation that can be dangerous for dogs. In this case, it was probably a big bear that was walking slowly and fighting the dogs as it walked. A big enough bear, my granddad explained, could easily hurt or kill the dogs, but couldn't be hurt by the dogs.

Although my granddad was a sizable man, he could move rapidly through the woods. But that day, he found the dogs and the bear in a terribly dense mountain laurel thicket that he couldn't make his way through. So instead, he improvised. He jumped as high as he could to try and see the bear. I could hear my granddad's enthusiasm as he was telling me this, almost as if I were there with him. "I jumped in the air, and oh my God," he said. "That was the biggest bear I'd ever seen."

He came up with a plan. The dogs were still baying—

or fighting—the bear, so he would jump again, but this time holding his favorite gun, the Winchester Model 12, a twelve-gauge shotgun loaded with slugs. He jumped, pointed the shotgun at the bear, and pulled the trigger.

"As I jumped in the air," he said, "*Bang!* Again and again, I jumped, until I had shot five times and the bear was dead." It took a large group of men to get the bear out of the woods and loaded into his truck. This was a very special bear to him, and he wanted my grandmother and the rest of the family to see it. So instead of taking the bear to the cabin to skin, as he usually did, he took it to the house. He backed up the truck to the front porch, hauled the bear inside, and dropped it onto the old farm table in the kitchen. Keep in mind this was a big family, so this was a big kitchen table. It was oval shaped and measured over eight feet long by four feet wide. My mom, Irene Thacker, often spoke of this sight. "You couldn't see any part of the table," she said, "because the bear was hanging off all sides."

I was a taxidermist for over twenty years, and in that time, I had seen several bears over five hundred pounds. One even weighed over six hundred pounds. To cover the table in my granddad's kitchen like that, I have no doubt that bear weighed at least six hundred pounds, and probably more. It could have even been a state record, had there been scales back then to weigh it. As my granddad skinned the bear that day, he found all five slug holes in the bear's hide. Still, I would love to have had that bear's skin. It would have made a great rug.

My granddad was an honest, God-fearing gentleman who loved his family and made an honest living working on his farm. He rarely got to the city. The closest one was Roanoke, Virginia. He did, however, occasionally have to go to Fincastle, Virginia, the Botetourt County seat, to pay taxes. One day, while driving in Fincastle, he was pulled over by a county deputy.

"What did I do wrong, officer?" Granddad asked, confused.

"Sir, you were going the wrong way down a one-way street."

My granddad, being very much rooted in the culture of Appalachia, had an honest reply ready. "Sir," he said, "I was only going one way."

A month or so later, he went to court.

My granddad never spoke to me about it, but my Aunt Cassie Lowe told me she had taken him to court that day. On the stand, tears poured down his cheeks as he told the judge the same thing he told the deputy, that he was only going one direction. The judge warned my granddad to be on the lookout for one-way signs and instructed my aunt to point one out to him on the way home. She told the judge that she had, in fact, already done this on the way over that morning.

"Mr. Conner," the judge said, "I'm not fining you for this, so you'll only need to pay the court costs." Yet after the judge dismissed him, my granddad continued to sit there, fresh tears rolling down his cheeks.

"Judge," my granddad croaked, "I need to confess to you what I did. This has been bothering me for many years." He proceeded to tell the judge of the time on his farm that his dogs had treed a bear. Even though he knew it was out of season, he had killed the bear. Sobbing, he continued telling the story of how he had searched around for the right stick and killed the bear as it came down from the tree.

The judge listened to my granddad's account, then spoke. "I can tell you've already paid for this a hundred times over, Mr. Conner," he said. "And I'm sure you'll never do anything like that again. I appreciate your honesty, sir. That will be all."

My granddad thanked him and left.

As a child, I couldn't wait until I was old enough to go bear hunting with my granddad, my hero. But as I got older, my granddad did, too.

One year, after hunting season had ended, my granddad sat me down. "It looks like you're old enough now," he said. "Why don't you come hunting with me next year?"

I was overjoyed. I couldn't wait for next fall to come. But by spring, my granddad was acting out of character, his memory was failing, and he was lashing out at people. That was not my loving granddad. In the summer of that year, he was diagnosed with hardening of the arteries. Sadly, due to his declining health, I never got to go bear hunting with my granddad. But he has forever remained my real-life Daniel Boone.

*This chapter is dedicated to my granddad,
Ernest Vaten Conner.*

CHAPTER 2

The Beginning

In the fall of 1990, I started a new adventure in life. I was hired as a paramedic for Carilion Patient Transport. By that time, I had been volunteering for ten years and had become an excellent paramedic.

Also, I went from hunting squirrels, which was the first animal I had ever killed, to hunting rabbits with my Uncle Paul Lowe. He had six long-legged Bluetick and beagle mix hounds, and they were some excellent rabbit beagles. While rabbit hunting, it was lots of fun to hit those rabbits as they zigged and zagged. Sometimes while rabbit hunting, the dogs would flush quail, that is, cause the birds to fly up out of the brush. There were plenty of quail back then. The first time the dogs flushed quail, I think my heart may have stopped for a few seconds. The sound of their wings could scare you if you weren't used to it.

Then I started deer hunting, and it became my new passion. In this chapter, you'll hear about some of the most memorable deer hunts I had as a teenager.

I was out hunting one day and saw a large herd of deer about two hundred yards away. They were making lots of noise and running toward me. In my experience, deer were usually quiet. But a big herd like that really made a lot of noise. The whole herd was headed straight in my direction. Then, about forty yards behind them, I spotted a buck. It had a rack that even from a distance looked enormous. I was sitting with my back against a tree, and I wasn't going to move until I had the shot on that big boy. As I sat there, one doe crossed over me at knee level as she ran. She didn't step on me, but if she had, I wouldn't have made a sound as it would have spooked the buck. Every single deer in the herd was a doe except the last one. Most of them were less than ten yards from me, but I sat still and put all my concentration into getting a shot at the big buck.

I normally hunted deer with a rifle, but that day I had a Remington Model 870 shotgun. Unlike with my rifle, I needed a close shot. The ground where I was sitting had a slight incline, but fifteen yards below me it dropped sharply down into the holler, where the deer were coming from.

I couldn't see the buck, but I could hear him walking. Then he stopped, and I could make out the tops of his antlers. Oh no, he's scented me, I thought. I may not get a shot on this big buck after all. He started walking again. *Stalk, stalk, stalk* is what I heard as he lumbered toward me. When he was ten yards from me, he turned, giving me the perfect side shot.

I was sixteen years old, and I had been taught in hunter's education never to disengage your gun's safety until you are ready to shoot, and I was about to find out the reason for that. I put the bead sight on the buck's shoulder, clicked the safety off, and was just about to squeeze off the shot when he about-faced, ready to run off, and my shot hit him in the hindquarters. I tried again. That pump sixteen-gauge shotgun sounded like an automatic going off as I placed the bead just in front of his shoulder and pulled the trigger. He went down onto his front knees. I ran over to him and put another shot in his neck, just to make sure he was dead. Later, after skinning the animal, I realized the last shot wasn't needed—his heart and lungs were filled with buckshot. It was a thirteen-point rack, the biggest deer I'd ever killed. I had it mounted.

Another year, on the opening day of bow season, I walked a mile and a half to find a place to set up my tree stand. I had been sitting there for about an hour and a half, and it was starting to get dark. I was about to leave, but I talked myself into staying five minutes longer. Moments later, I heard something coming toward me, but couldn't see what it was. By the time it was about twenty yards from me, I could see it was a nice-sized buck. Because it was getting dark, it was hard to see the deer through the peep sight on my bow. He was coming straight at me, which was not the shot I wanted but the only shot I had. I took aim anyway and let the arrow fly. It looked like a good shot. The buck whipped around and ran back up the hill. I could tell by the way he was running that he had been hit hard. He ran to the top of the ridge, maybe forty yards, and that's when I heard the death crash—the sound an animal makes when it falls to the ground and thrashes around for a few seconds before it dies. I am so glad he didn't go off the back side of the ridge because it would have been much harder to drag him away. When I climbed down from my stand, I paced off the distance to where I had shot him: eighteen yards. He turned out to be just an average-sized buck, an eight-pointer.

As I set out on the mile-and-a-half drag back to my truck, I fell, dropping my flashlight and losing all the batteries. I fumbled around for them and found all but one. Boy, that was a fun drag in the dark. I didn't get back to my truck until after 9:30.

On my ride out through the national forest road, I saw a vehicle coming in the opposite direction. It was my mom, Irene Joyce Conner Thacker, and my dad, Earl Legar Thacker. My wife, Judy Cauley, was also with them. This was before the days of cell phones, and since it was much later than I normally headed home, they were worried I had fallen out of my tree stand.

I ordered a white-tailed deer video kit that showed me how to mount this bow-kill, eight-point buck. It turned out looking like a deer, or at least I thought it had, so I decided to start my own small business as a taxidermist. The first year was slow. I mounted only four deer and charged 150 dollars each. In the fall of the following year, I received an invitation to attend the annual Virginia Taxidermists Association convention and competition. I was asked to bring some of my work to be judged. I felt so honored to be asked, especially since it was my first time going, so I took my best deer head to the convention. But the moment I walked into the showroom and started looking at the competition, I realized I really didn't know anything about taxidermy. My deer looked like a stuffed deer, but I learned what real taxidermy should look like. The mounted animal, I found out, should look as though it were still alive.

But what I enjoyed most about the competition were the numerous seminars. I learned so much that first year, and over the next year, I mounted twenty deer, some fish, and a few small game animals. I was pleased my animals were now looking much more alive.

The following year was the World Taxidermy Association Seminar and Competition in Georgia. I felt lucky it was close enough to drive to, because it could have been held anywhere in the world. So we loaded up my van with stuffed animals, and off we went. When we got there, I saw animals from all over the world. There were lions, tigers, and all kinds of African animals, including some I didn't even know existed. If you're an animal enthusiast and ever have a chance to go to a world show, I highly recommend it. The animals looked like they were alive and staring right back at me. This was world-class taxidermy.

I attended all the seminars I could fit into my schedule. They had classes like how to mount deer and how to paint fish. But as it happened, the best seminar I attended wasn't showing me how to mount anything. It was about how to run a successful taxidermy studio, presented by a world-famous whitetail taxidermist. During the class, he gave us the tools we needed to excel and make money in taxidermy. I will always remember him saying, "Would you rather mount four hundred deer heads for two hundred dollars, or two hundred deer heads for four hundred dollars?" The cash works out to be the same, but you would have to buy twice as many supplies—and spend twice as much time—mounting four hundred deer heads. He said all you need to do is spend a little more money and put in an extra hour or so on each mount to make it stand out from the others.

But your customer, he explained, won't be aware of all

this extra work. All he will see is a stuffed deer head. So when your customer comes to pick up the finished product, you have to be a good salesperson and point out all the extras you did. This is like training your customer, because now he is going to be looking at the finer points of every deer head he sees. That customer's word of mouth will send you more business, and you'll be able to get top dollar for your work.

That year, my business had grown from the year before. But my name wasn't out there yet. I put in a lot of extra work that year in the hopes word about me would spread, and it did.

That was also the year a friend of mine brought me an albino squirrel to mount. It had a pink nose and pink eyes, and it was so beautiful. I had known Rob Cook for several years. We both volunteered at the Troutville Rescue Squad and Fire Department. We sat there talking about the past, and of course, hunting. Before I knew it, he told me he had started bear hunting a couple of years ago and asked if I would like to go with him the very next day. There were only three days left in the season. I said I would love to, then told him about my granddad and how by the time I was old enough to go hunting with him, his health was failing, and I thought I would never get to fulfill my childhood dream. We planned to meet at five the next morning at Rob's house, about eight miles from mine.

The next morning, I got up at four, feeling tired. So excited was I about living out my childhood dream of bear hunting, I had hardly slept. I got into my two-wheel drive Ford F-150 and headed over to Rob's. There was more than a foot of snow on the ground, but fortunately the main roads were clear.

And then I got to his driveway. He lived on a steep hill, and his driveway was slick with packed snow. Even though I only had a two-wheel drive vehicle, I went for it. When I hit the driveway, I started spinning, so I cut the wheel hard to the left and parked in his yard.

Rob was up and had his black-and-tan dog, Hobo, already loaded in the dog box in the back of his black Chevy pickup. I threw my stuff in, and off we went. He explained that we were headed up to Bald Mountain in Craig County. That sounded great to me. I knew where Craig County was, but I had no idea where Bald Mountain was.

We drove onto Lignite Road, which runs up Bald Mountain. It was covered in packed snow, so we stopped to put chains on the tires before heading up the road. At the top, we went right at a fork in the road, which took us to South Prong, a small branch of Barbours Creek. We didn't go far before we encountered a long, straight swag—low area—in the road, where Rob parked his truck.

Other vehicles were parked there, too. We hopped out, and Rob introduced me to David Ward (we called him Fox), Richard Trent (who went by Gusto), Brian Wright (nickname Striker), and Jason "Soccer Man" Guilliams. We talked for a few minutes and decided to head up the old logging road that led across the top of mountain.

As daylight broke, the guys unloaded their dogs, placing two dogs on each lead. That's when I noticed their collars were different from anything I had seen before in that they each had an antenna attached. I asked what this was, and Rob said that each collar had a different radio frequency. He produced a little blue box, made by Wildlife Materials, Inc., with a folding Yagi antenna hooked up. It was beeping, and he explained that you could tell where each dog was by pointing it in different directions and listening for the loudest beeps. I was amazed. All I knew was my granddad needed a small army of men lined up in the woods to hear the dogs.

Excited to get the chase on, we walked up the logging road a ways. I was leading two dogs who were pulling so hard I could barely hold on. Moments later, they slipped away from me and bounded up a small ridge, still tied together.

"You gotta hold on tight to those dogs," Gusto said. "And you'd better go get them fast because they could hang themselves with that lead still attached."

I bolted up the ridge and was able to catch them about a hundred yards up. Boy, did I hold on tight to that lead the rest of the day.

We had trekked a mile and a half—through sixteen inches of snow—when Cindy, one of Fox's dogs, started to bark. He told me Cindy was their strike dog, the lead dog that would bark when it smelled a bear. The best strike dogs would not bark on anything except the animal you were hunting, which was good, because when bear hunting, you didn't want to be running deer.

Cindy was moving slowly with just an occasional bark. From what my granddad told me, I guessed this was a cold trail, and Rob confirmed it was. Cindy was moving in the same direction we were, but she stayed a few hundred yards left of the road. Her slow bawls became more frequent until soon they were more like barks than long, drawn-out bawls. When I heard Cindy barking as fast as she could, I knew she had a hot track and may even be looking at the bear.

We started cutting in—releasing—one dog at a time. Rob set Hobo loose while I released Dixie, a beautiful, brindle-colored Plott Hound, and one other. We would release them one at a time and let them get about two hundred yards out on the trail before cutting in the next dog.

Soon we had released all the dogs, and wow, the excitement of hearing them and knowing they were chasing a bear was overwhelming. We walked in their direction while we could still hear them, but as they moved farther away, it got harder to hear. At that point, Fox pulled out his blue box, hooked his Yagi antenna up to it, and pointed it around. It produced a faint *beep beep* when he pointed it off either side of the trail, but when he pointed it straight down the trail, it gave off a much louder beep. "They're still straight ahead of us," Fox declared, "but they may be slightly off to the left side."

We topped out on a high knoll where we could hear the dogs again. They were indeed off to the left side now, and the barking wasn't as intense as it had been earlier. As we sat there, two of the dogs appeared and strolled toward us, not barking. "There are some steep rocks in the area where we last heard the dogs," Rob said, "so the bear probably lost the dogs going down through that."

We were now just hearing an occasional bark, and the dogs were coming back to us. Still, with a couple of dogs loose, we continued alongside the mountain to get them and hopefully hit another track. In about a half mile, we had rounded up all the dogs, but after walking another two miles, we didn't hear a peep from any of them. We decided to call it a day and head back to the trucks.

Fox asked if I had enjoyed my first day bear hunting. Smiling ear to ear, I told him I'd had an awesome day. We decided same time, same place for the next morning.

Like the previous morning, I was up by four, and slip-sliding into Rob's driveway by five. Off we went to Bald Mountain again. We put on the chains as soon as we reached Lignite Road, then continued up the mountain to the swag.

As we parked, I noticed a truck that hadn't been there the day before. A man got out and introduced himself as Malcolm Horne. He said he had his own hunting group, but none of them could hunt today. We asked if he'd like to go with us, and he said he'd love to.

At daybreak, we led the dogs out onto the trail. We had walked less than half a mile when all the dogs absolutely blew up, barking at the top of their lungs. It was deafening, and—oh my God—those dogs were pulling me as hard as they could. If only I had a sleigh, I thought. That was the day I learned I could wrap their leads around a tree to slow them down.

We cut Cindy loose first, then Fox told us to cut them all loose. We didn't hesitate. Ten seconds later, they were off. Wow, the ring of those dogs. This was definitely a hot track, and I knew this was the day I would see my first bear in the wild. The dogs were a few hundred yards up the trail when they suddenly changed direction. Now they were running back toward us full cry, meaning they were barking as fast as they could. I was so excited. Seconds later, a cub bounded down the mountain about fifty yards away from me, with two of the dogs right behind it, ready to catch it.

Rob's eyes widened. "Round up all the dogs!" he yelled,

seeing what was about to happen.

I sprinted toward the first two dogs, but it was too late: Dixie had already jumped on top of the cub as it lay on its back in the snow. The cub, which probably weighed about fifty pounds, was trying to bite the dog. I grabbed Dixie, but the two animals were in a death lock with each other. I had Dixie's collar in one hand and the loose skin of her back in the other. I managed to lift her up, but the cub came with her. I didn't want to injure either animal, but I needed to pry them apart. I shook Dixie as hard as I could.

Finally, after all the shaking and yelling, I managed to separate them and put Dixie back on her lead. The cub took off running and the other dogs ran after it, closing in fast. In the blink of an eye, the bear treed. I was amazed at how quickly the cub clambered up there. By now we had caught most of the dogs, with three still at the base of the tree barking. But the dogs weren't just sitting there, they were standing on hind legs, front paws on the tree, jumping in the air and doing everything they could to get to the cub. Wow, the excitement of seeing my first bear treed.

But Rob wasn't quite as impressed. "Let's move on up the mountain and try to find a bigger bear," he said. We called off the dogs and put them on leads, then walked up past where we had been the previous day.

We didn't get any new strikes that day, but as we headed back to the truck and drove off, I knew I had found my new passion in life. From that day on, deer hunting never meant as much to me. I had become a bear hunter.

Since the following day was the last day of the season, we decided to go again the next morning. We didn't know exactly where yet, but it would be somewhere on Bald Mountain.

At three a.m., my phone rang. It was Rob, telling me to get to his house in a half hour or he would be leaving without me. That was an hour and a half earlier than what we had planned. I didn't know what was going on, but Rob was already in his truck when I arrived. I grabbed my gear and jumped in with him. As we headed to Bald Mountain, he explained that Gusto, who had spent the night in his cabin on top of the mountain, had gone out to a bar Friday evening. As he was coming back home around midnight, he discovered a bear track that wasn't there when he had left.

"It's a good-sized track, too," Rob said. "And Gusto told me all four of its tracks had blood in them, which means the bear's pads are worn and bleeding. Obviously, the bear's been run a lot this season."

As we had done on previous mornings, we put the chains on Rob's tires and up the mountain we went. Instead of turning right when we got to the crossroads, as we had two days before, we kept straight. A little farther up the road, we found Gusto and Fox.

Gusto was concerned that other hunters would come along and try to get our bear. "I'd like to put our trucks on this track," he said, "so no one will cut their dogs loose on this track we're starting."

As daylight broke, we took the dogs out of the truck. Our first step was to walk the track and find where the bear had bedded down for the night. The tracks led off to the right side of the mountain, basically right behind Gusto's cabin. We started down off the mountain, which was covered in thick pine and mountain laurel. The farther down we went, the thicker it got. Soon we were trudging through blackberry bushes. Then we ran into our worst nightmare: a thicket of greenbrier. If you don't know what greenbrier is, it's a plant with an almost inch-long briar and a stem so tough you can't break it like you can blackberry vines.

The dogs seemed like they were onto something all the way down. It was a cold track, but when we got close to the bottom of the holler, the dogs started barking and pulling hard as the track heated up. The going was slow because the dogs kept getting tangled in all the briars. I wanted to let the dogs loose, but we continued on.

Minutes later, we found the spot where the bear had bedded down in the thicket—but no bear. I'm sure it had heard us coming. Since it clearly hadn't been gone long, we cut Cindy loose and she charged off like she was on fire. When she was about a hundred yards away, we cut the next dog loose, and so on, until they were all at full cry heading toward South Prong. By the time all of us had fought our way through the laurel and greenbrier and made it to the road on South Prong, Fox was there waiting for us. He told us the dogs had now crossed over the mountain and we could drive to catch up with them. They were moving slowly now, and I knew from my granddad's stories that meant they were walking the bear.

A couple of the hunters jumped into Fox's truck and rode up front with him, while the others—including me, being the new kid—climbed onto his dog box in the back. Rob was with me and told me to hold on. We drove about five miles along a dirt and gravel road, then we turned right onto Barbours Creek Road, which was paved. Wow, what a ride.

At that moment, I was grateful for the rig, the rack on top of the dog box. It consisted of an aluminum frame that could attach one to three dogs, allowing them to pick up scents and strike a bear track while driving on a forest road. I wished there was a harness to fasten *me* to the rig, but instead I just held on for dear life as we hung a right onto the hardtop road. Now, rather than averaging twenty to thirty miles per hour, we were doing fifty to sixty. Damn, was it cold on the back of that truck.

After about two miles, we slowed down. Rob explained that Fox was trying to get a location fix on the dogs. We rumbled to a stop, and Fox turned off the engine. I was expecting to hear the dogs at full cry, but I heard nothing. We all jumped out of the truck and listened. We knew the dogs were nearby, but we didn't hear a sound. So Rob grabbed his own tracking box, and Gusto, Soccer Man, and I followed him into the woods. The laurels were thick, but at least there were no greenbriers, thank goodness.

We trekked across a flat to the base of the mountain, where we spotted Dixie, who looked injured by the way she was walking. Some of the other Plott Hounds showed up, and we put them on leashes so we could attend to Dixie. When we examined her, we found a large, gaping wound over her right rib cage. Rob picked her up and carried her out to the truck while the rest of us stayed back to look for the other dogs. Before long, we had found most of them, including Cindy. Fortunately, none of the others were injured. We looked around some more and found where the fight with the bear had taken place, along with a trail of bear prints that went back up the mountain where they had just come down.

"Let's get the dogs back on the track," Gusto said. But even after we put her nose directly on the track, Cindy made it clear she wasn't interested. Gusto figured it was because of the fight. "She must have been smacked pretty good if she doesn't want to go back on that track."

We decided to follow the track a ways to see if the dogs would start back on it. But as we climbed, we didn't hear one peep from the dogs. It was only after we had hiked half a mile that Cindy finally sniffed out the track. We smiled. A hundred feet later, she let out a long bawl. Gusto let her go, and she went out on the track, which was already an hour old. We waited for her to get several hundred yards away before cutting the next dog loose. Then, every two to three hundred yards, the remaining dogs were cut in. We advised Fox on our handheld CB radio that all the dogs were back on the bear. Fox said he would keep track of the dogs, then informed us that Rob had taken Dixie to the veterinarian but promised to come right back. He had taken a closer look at Dixie back at the truck and discovered she had several broken ribs and a punctured lung.

As we continued climbing the mountain, Gusto told me and Soccer Man to go on ahead. In addition to being a little older, he'd also had a knee replacement and couldn't keep up with us.

Soccer Man and I, now on our own, had just topped the mountain when Fox told us that another bear hunting group had joined with our dogs. He said they had seen our dogs walking the bear on top of the mountain. Fox thought that was a good idea, so he made an announcement over the CB that any other hunting groups should pack with our dogs and go after this bear because it had seriously hurt one of our dogs. According to Fox, the other hunters had already put twenty hounds on the bear, which meant we had a total of thirty or so hounds in the woods and on the chase.

We couldn't hear the dogs, and since Rob had taken the tracking box with him, we had no way to find them. We thought about cutting down to the road to regroup, but Fox told us to stay on top of the mountain and walk toward where we had treed the cub the day before. That was about two miles, but fortunately the walking was a little easier now since the top of the mountain was relatively flat with only some smaller hills to climb.

As we walked, Fox informed Soccer Man that the dogs had come down off the mountain and were heading into the huge holler near the white rocks. That's when we heard the far-off roar of the dogs, although it was so faint we could barely hear it.

We started down the mountain, and soon we were at the logging road, past the swag where the cub had treed the day before. We could hear the dogs better, but they were still probably a mile and a half from us. It sounded like they were treeing and not on the move. At that moment, Fox told us to get in there as quickly as we could, saying even though they were stopped, he thought they were baying, not treeing, because there were no treeing switches going off on the collars. These were switches built in to the collars that knew when a dog was looking up a tree and would send out a double beep instead of the normal sound.

We were going so hard that I slipped and fell and hit my right knee on a rock. Damn, that hurt. Even though my knee was in pain and had begun to swell, I kept up the pace with Soccer Man right beside me. The dogs were now at full cry, about five hundred yards from us, and I knew without a doubt we were going to kill this bear. Soccer Man informed Fox that he was going to turn off his radio since we were getting close. That was because if a bear were to hear a radio close by, it could suddenly jump, slide down a tree, or, if it was being bayed by the dogs, run off.

Now, just two hundred yards from us, fifteen to twenty of the dogs had the bear surrounded. What a sight! Some of the dogs were ten feet or so in front of the bear, others were at its sides, and a few of the dogs had grabbed ahold of the bear's fur, tugging at it.

Just then, the bear whipped around and swiped at the dogs behind him. Those dogs backed away, while the dogs that were now behind the bear began chewing on his ass-end. This was such a sight to see—nothing like the cub from the day before. We were now a hundred yards away. I had my Winchester Model 670 .30-06 strapped to me, and I took it off and got ready to shoot.

"We have to get closer," Soccer Man warned. "We have to pick the right time to shoot, or we could end up killing a dog."

At that moment, the bear took off down the mountain and ran several hundred yards. Then it turned and headed down low onto what Soccer Man told me was leased land. We communicated this to Fox over the radio, and he told us to come out to Lignite Road, which was about a mile's hike.

When we reached his truck, he informed us that the dogs had crossed back over the mountain to Barbours Creek, which meant it was time for another drive. Soccer Man hopped up front, and I got back on the dog box. I knew this wasn't going to be a fun ride. We had five miles to go to where we had first caught a ride that morning. Being soaked with sweat, I was already freezing by the time we reached the paved road, and I knew it would only get worse as we sped up. When we got back to where Dixie had been injured, I was expecting to slow down, but oh no: full speed ahead.

We drove three more miles before we came to a stop. To our left was Nicholls Knob, a part of Potts Mountain, and we could hear a couple of the dogs climbing the knob. Fox said that Cindy had already crossed the mountain. Soccer Man got out of the truck to go after the dogs, and Fox and I continued down the road a few more miles and took a left into Rich Patch. After another half mile and another left turn, Fox's tracker was beeping, telling me we were on the right path. The dogs, he said, were up in what was called the Children's Forest. We drove another mile into the national forest, where he pulled up to a bar gate and parked the truck. In front of us, we could hear the dogs yapping.

"Go kill that damn bear," Fox said, passing me a handheld radio.

I was drawing nearer to the dogs when they took a turn and started moving farther away. I continued in their direction, walking for maybe a mile into the Children's Forest when Fox called me on the radio and said I may as well come out because the dogs were now crossing back to the top of Potts Mountain toward Barbours Creek. It was now less than an hour before dark, making me think this bear wasn't going to be killed this year.

At this point, I was drained, mentally and physically. My knee hurt—actually, I think every part of my body hurt—and it was official: this had been my hardest day ever in the woods. I walked back with not much pep in my step. Back at the truck, Fox gave me the news he had heard over the radio: eight or so other hunting groups had put every dog they owned on this bear, and throughout the day, close to two hundred dogs had been released to chase it. I was in total amazement of this. What a day it had been.

But it was now dark, and the hunt was over. Feeling defeated, we headed back toward Barbours Creek. About a mile up the road, just past where Soccer Man had gone up, we got a faint beep on Cindy, so we went up the road to locate her as the beeping grew louder.

At that moment, the radio crackled to life with two words: "Bear dead." It sounded like Soccer Man. We congratulated him, but we heard nothing back, so we tried to reach him several more times. Fearing he may have been injured, we got back in line with Cindy, who was straight up the mountain from us, because Fox thought Soccer Man and the other dogs would be on top or just over the top.

"Radio dead," came Soccer Man's voice over the CB just then.

We breathed a sigh of relief knowing he was okay. Gusto had now caught up with us, and he and I started up the mountain to track Cindy. Some hunters from other groups also joined us. At the top of the mountain, we found Soccer Man, where he had all the dogs tied up. He pointed down the mountain and told us the bear was a few hundred yards down the slope. The easiest way to get the bear out, he told us, was to drag it downhill to a small stream, and then follow the stream out to the paved road. Although it would be a longer drag, it would be mostly downhill.

Soccer Man told us the story of what happened. When he first topped out, he could hear the dogs, so he headed down to them in the Children's Forest. Then he heard them moving up the mountain again, so he hurried back up. As he crossed the top of the mountain, he knew he was getting closer to them.

Then he saw the bear, along with Cindy about ten feet behind it. The bear was just a few hundred yards away, so Soccer Man perched in a tree and squeezed the trigger of his .270 Winchester rifle. The bear fell in its tracks. But his radio died before he could tell us about the kill, so he turned it off and waited about thirty minutes before turning it back on. He keyed up and said, "Bear dead," but the radio beeped and immediately died again, which was why he never replied to us. After about twenty minutes, he was able to turn it back on and tell us about his radio problem.

Knowing that somewhere around two hundred dogs had been released throughout the day, I was expecting to see lots of dogs there. But there were only seven or eight. In fact, the only dog still on the bear when it was killed was Cindy. She had started the chase and was the only dog that had finished the chase. The rest of the dogs were from other groups of bear hunters. For a twelve-year-old dog, that was not a bad day. Of the eight hunters on the mountain, two of them took all the dogs back down to the road we had come in on, and the rest of us started the mile-and-a-half drag out.

Rob was now back from the vet. Fox had found a phone to call the game warden to tell him we had killed a bear and wouldn't be out of the mountains before the check station closed. So instead, the game warden came over to us to check the bear. It was a hard drag; the creek was overgrown with mountain laurel, and it was after ten p.m. before we made it to the hardtop road.

There, we found a group of other bear hunters waiting to take a look at the bear's paws. They wanted to see if this was the same bear we had started, or if we had killed the bear they started. All the bear's pads were deeply worn from all the running it had done that season. Malcolm Horne, whom we had met earlier, stepped up to inspect the bear's paws.

"Well, boys, that is y'all's bear," he declared. "That is without a doubt the bear you started." He then congratulated us on a job well done. When some of the other hunters objected, Malcolm, being quite a respected bear hunter, put a hush to all that talk.

What a day. It had started at three in the morning, and now it was past ten at night. I arrived home at midnight and just knew I would pass out the moment my head hit the pillow. But no. Due to total exhaustion, I couldn't sleep. I tossed and turned all night and got an hour of shuteye at most.

The next day, I figured it out: I had walked somewhere between twenty and twenty-five miles, and that was up the steepest mountains and through the thickest vegetation. No wonder I was so exhausted. Later, we met up to skin and butcher the bear, and I was given some of the meat to take home.

Those three days gave me a new passion, bear hunting. I know my granddad was looking down on me and smiling that I had taken on his passion in life—the only relative to do so. His sons, my Uncle Riley and Uncle Lee, had gone once or twice with him and said they couldn't keep up with their dad. My cousin Ernest Guilliams, eight years older than me, went with him once, and he, too, decided it wasn't his cup of tea. My Uncle Paul, the best deer hunter I've ever known, once joined Granddad and also found bear hunting not to his liking.

I'm here to say it takes a special breed of person to go bear hunting and enjoy it. Throughout my years, I can't tell you how many big, bad, tough deer hunters were so excited to go with us, itching to kill a bear, then hunt with us for one day and decide that was all they could handle. You need to have a burning love for the sport, or be stupid, to seek out the abuse of a long, hard day in the mountains hunting bears. Thank you, Rob Cook, for my new passion in life.

CHAPTER 3
The Loss of Cindy

Because the last day of the previous season had just about killed me, I resolved to get myself into better shape for the next season. I started eating healthier. I purchased a new ten-speed bike to build leg strength and stamina. I worked hard that spring and summer. I was determined to be ready for many more long days of bear hunting.

In August, training season came in. During training season, we weren't allowed to carry guns. It was just a chance to train the dogs and tune them up before hunting season started. New puppies, having never seen a bear before, could start their live training, while the other dogs got much-needed exercise, as it would have been over eight months since they last chased a bear.

Training new puppies to hunt started when they were old enough to eat on their own, usually at the age of three weeks. To start, I would place a small amount of soft food on a rag and drag it across the floor, leaving small niblets along the way. This helped the puppy learn to use its nose to find food. A meal would be waiting for the puppy about six feet away, and every couple of days, I would increase the distance. I would also move everything around each day to make sure the puppy was actually using its nose, not just going in the same direction out of habit.

Once the puppy knew how to sniff out its food, it was time to introduce it to a bear. Well, not an actual bear, but a square of bear hide, about a foot on each side. To make it realistic, I applied bear scent to the hide, which got the puppy used to the way a bear smelled. The puppies loved to play and roughhouse with it like a toy.

After a few days of playing, it was time to step up the training. I would drag the bear hide along the floor just as I had with the food. However, I would use a rope to do this to avoid touching the hide and contaminating it with my own scent. Just as before, a meal would be waiting for the puppy at the end. Then, after each training session, I would place the hide in a zip lock bag to preserve the scent.

When the puppy was old enough to be outside, we started doing longer training hunts. As a new hunter, the puppy needed to learn it must hunt for its meals. By now, the puppy could follow a hot trail and find its food in no time at all, so I would set up a cold trail to make it harder. But there was an easier way to do this than waiting for hours to let the trail cool down: instead of continuously dragging the hide across the ground, I would pick it up every few feet and carry it, then set it down again. Since there were now breaks in the trail, the puppy had to work its nose harder to stay on track and find the food. As the puppy got better at tracking, the gaps grew longer.

The next phase was training the puppy to tree. At the end of the trail, I would hang the scented bear hide several feet up in a tree. No food, just the hide. When the puppy found the hide and had its paws on the tree trying to get at it, I would give it the food as a reward and say, "Good doggie," while petting the animal. It was a great reward because dogs love to be petted.

Finally, it was August of my first training season. Knowing I'd be seeing bears up close and personal, I initially had some apprehension about not having a gun with me, but I was assured that black bears weren't the same as grizzly or brown bears in that they wouldn't attack you for no reason.

However, there were still two reasons a black bear would attack. The first was if you found yourself between the sow—female bear—and her cubs. The second was if you happened to be in the bear's only path of escape. In that case, it wouldn't be attacking you per se, but it could run you over in its attempt to escape. Learning how to avoid a black bear attack made me feel a little better.

On opening day of training season, we had permission to hunt the leased land we had skirted around the previous year. We drove up through the property with a couple of dogs on Fox's rig. Moments later, we got a hot strike, and we let the two dogs on top of the rig go. They hit the trail full cry, so we opened all our dog boxes, and the chase was on. I also cut in my first bear dog, a beautiful Redbone Coonhound named Rusty. It was my first time letting my own dog loose on a bear. The dogs sounded awesome. I'd missed hearing them.

By now, the dogs were halfway up the mountain, and we couldn't hear them anymore. Moments later, all the treeing switches went off, and Fox told us we had the bear. Gusto, Striker, Rob, and I headed to where the dogs had treed the bear, which was about a mile away. Fortunately, all the training I had done to get in shape was paying off. I felt great, even after climbing over several steep and overgrown finger ridges.

As we hiked, the treeing switches continued to tell us the dogs were "looking up the bush," as we sometimes said. Our tracking box indicated we were very close now, even though we could only hear an occasional bark, which was odd. Coming over the top of the last finger ridge, there were the dogs, only fifty yards from us, at full cry, up against a rock bluff. The bluff, apparently, had dampened their barking, which explained why we had trouble hearing them.

The bear was about eight feet up in the tree. Rob guessed he wouldn't stay treed for long at that height. Usually, he said, they feel safer if they climb much higher and are farther from the dogs. Sure enough, just as we moved toward the tree, the bear jumped down and landed in the middle of the dog pack, and the chase was on again. I was thrilled to see this amazing scene, a bear leaping into a pack of dogs.

The dogs chased the bear down the mountain, then turned back in the direction we had started the chase, just a little lower on the mountain. From our post atop a high knoll on the finger ridge, we could hear the whole chase. Rusty sat beside me as we settled in to listen.

Rusty was about two and hadn't been hunted or trained much. He was also hard to catch, as I found out. He much preferred being loose, doing his own thing. Gusto suggested I put him on his lead, and if the bear treed again, we could take him to the tree and let him see his first bear.

As we listened, the dogs' tone changed, and the treeing switches went off again. We keyed up the radio to tell Fox the dogs had treed, probably just below where he was. We scrambled down the mountain toward the tree. Fox, meanwhile, had driven into the woods and told us he was now turning off his radio. That meant he was getting close. Minutes later, Fox told us the bear had jumped down and was heading toward Lignite Road. He hopped into his truck to go and find the dogs.

As we headed back to our trucks, Fox was already out of the leased land and almost to Lignite Road. When we reached our trucks, Fox had a fix on the dogs. They were on the "rough road," he said. I didn't know where this rough road was, so I followed the gang out of the lease, onto the hardtop road, and turned right. After half a mile, we took a right on Lignite Road and drove up to the base of Bald Mountain.

To our left was a narrow dirt road that wound between Bald Mountain to our right and Little Mountain to our left. Fox said the bear was about a mile down that road. The road was rugged, with plenty of steep stretches and muddy patches, which made me grateful for my four-wheel drive vehicle. When we caught up with Fox, the dogs were hammering about five hundred yards away up the side of Bald Mountain.

This bear already had a nickname: Jumping Bear, because it wouldn't climb very far up trees before jumping down. This made it very hard for us to get, so we switched up our strategy. This time, only one person would approach the tree, and the rest of us would stay a few hundred yards back. Rob went first and was able to get under the tree. The rest of us followed, and I was treated to a sight I would remember forever: Jumping Bear, six feet up in the tree, had climbed out onto a limb and was lying on it, swiping at the dogs. The dogs were going nuts. They were jumping as high as they could to get to the bear. The bear was just out of reach of the dogs, and they just out of reach of the bear. We, too, remained just out of swiping distance as we watched. This was the coolest thing I had ever seen. We enjoyed the sight for a good twenty minutes.

I had led Rusty in to see his first bear, but he didn't seem all that impressed. He hung back twenty feet from all the action. I tried to bring him closer, but I couldn't catch him. And when it came time to round up all the dogs, again, dang dog wouldn't let me catch him. Rob told me Rusty would probably follow us, and he was right, but when we reached the truck, it still took another five minutes to collar him.

Meanwhile, Cindy looked awfully tired. Walking her out had been slow going. We took a closer look at her. We didn't find any injuries, but it sure looked like Cindy was beginning to show her age.

During that training season, we treed three or four more bears, but none were as dramatic as Jumping Bear. Most would climb thirty to fifty feet up the tree. I no longer had any apprehension about being there without a gun. It was just fun now: enjoying nature, seeing bears up in trees, hearing our hounds running. I was learning so much about bear hunting. I still wished I could have hunted with my hero, my granddad.

It was now December, bear hunting season. I had had a great time seeing a few bears during chase season, and I had also enjoyed a good deer season. But now I was ready to kill my first bear. Our first stop was the swag where we had hunted last season. We parked and put all the dogs on leads.

Cindy looked better after taking a couple of months off. She seemed to have more pep in her step as we walked along the logging road. Then, Cindy let out a bawl at almost the same spot where we had struck a bear the very first day I was here. We cut her loose, and she headed off in the same direction she had last time. As soon as one dog went out a hundred yards, we cut another one loose. The track was warmer than it had been the last time we were here, and the dogs sounded great. But like last time, they soon fell out of earshot. I was hoping to have a tracking box of my own by next season, but for now, Rob was tracking for us.

We continued along the logging road until we could hear the dogs again, only now, it sounded like they were moving in three or four different directions. Rob surmised that either a sow and her cubs had split off in different directions, or the bear had lost the dogs, and the dogs were trying to figure out where it had gone. This was the same area the bear had lost them last time. As we listened, the barking dwindled down, and some of the dogs came back to us.

After we rounded them all up, we saw no sign of Cindy. Rob thought she might be down at the rocks, which was where bears usually lost dogs. That was exactly where we found her. She was moving, but very slowly. We checked her out and saw no injuries, so we figured old age was finally catching up with her. After we led her back up from the rocks, she took a few steps, then lay down.

We ended up carrying her off the mountain that day. Fox took her to the vet, who also found no injuries and confirmed she was suffering from old age. Later that week, Cindy died. She would be missed—but at that time we had no idea just how much.

We continued hunting without Cindy, our strike dog. We tried out several others as strike dogs, starting with Dixie, who had recovered from her lung and rib injuries. But each time, it didn't go as well as it had with Cindy. The dogs seemed unorganized, and more often than not, it felt like a dog chase more than a bear hunt.

We needed a good strike dog, so Rob did some research and located a Treeing Walker Coonhound out west that sounded like a good prospect. Rob had the dog, a lighter-color walker, shipped to him, and he named her Magic. By now it was toward the end of the season, but since Magic had been previously hunted on bears and mountain lions, we were hopeful we could get a bear or two. But as it turned out, the season wasn't meant to be as we'd hoped.

During the off season, we loaded up and headed to Salisbury, North Carolina, for Walker Days. This was a huge event where all kinds of dogs were sold, and vendors peddled their hunting gear. I was looking for a wildlife tracking box, a Yagi antenna, and a collar. The box I found was about two inches square by eight inches long, with a pouch that attached to my belt. This small size was much easier to carry in the mountains. We bought new leads and collars, along with bear scent for training. We had a great time at Walker Days.

Around that time, I was contacted by a Mr. Creed, a coon hunter who had a large, dark-colored walker with long legs. He asked if I would be interested in him. I said yes and went over to pick up the dog. His name was Wahoo. Mr. Creed told me that the people he hunted with didn't want Wahoo near their dogs because he could be a little snippy under a tree. What a beautiful dog he was, though. With a new dog and new tracking equipment, I was stoked for training season to start.

We treed several bears that season. I no longer had Rusty. He had gone to a friend of mine, who said he would like to give Rusty a try coon hunting. Magic, Rob's dog, was doing an awesome job, and it was nice to see bears up the bush again. For my part, I was very happy with Wahoo. Those long legs made him extremely fast, and we never had a problem with him being snippy at any tree. Best of all, I had only paid fifty dollars for him. What a deal!

That season, we hunted the Hoop Hole Trail, which adjoined the leased land farther down past Bald Mountain. True to its name, the trail made a large circle, or hoop. It went about halfway up the mountain, where another hoop ran to the top and made a figure eight–shaped path. From the top, it was about twelve miles to the swag on top of Bald Mountain.

With its steep terrain and bubbling mountain stream full of native trout, Hoop Hole Trail was a bear's paradise. In my younger days, my friend Joe Maxie and I had fished that stream a number of times. With native trout, we had to be very quiet and sneak up on them or they wouldn't bite. They also weren't very big. The largest one I caught measured about seven inches. (By the way, one of the best ways to eat native trout is to fry them in flour. It's delicious, and the bones become soft enough that you can eat the whole fish, bones and all.)

A lot of the stream wasn't fishable because of the thick mountain laurel that surrounded it, where crawling on hands and knees was the only way to get through it. But it was in a thicket just like this one that my granddad had shot the huge bear while jumping in the air.

From the parking lot at Hoop Hole Trail, we headed up the mountain. We got a strike within minutes and released the dogs, spacing them apart on the track. They sounded good as they moved toward the top. But then, Cassie and Hobo cut to the right to cross the finger ridge there. At this point, tracking down along the creek was difficult due to steep terrain that blocked the signal, so we continued up the mountain to the center of the figure eight, where we could get a tracking fix on all the dogs. Magic, Dixie, and Wahoo were showing treed up the mountain and to the left. But Cassie and Hobo, both of whom were Rob's, were back down in the direction we had just been. We decided to go up to where the other dogs had the bear treed, then go back for Cassie and Hobo later.

In the tree, we found a sow and a cub. The sow was about twenty feet up, sitting in a notch, and the cub was ten feet above her, lying on a thick branch with its legs dangling off both sides of the limb. This was my first time seeing two bears in a tree. Because it was still early in training season, the cub was only about forty pounds. We sat there for a while, listening to the dogs and observing the bears in the tree. Then we leashed up the dogs and set off to find Cassie and Hobo. The tracking box still showed them in the same direction as before.

Down at the short loop, we tracked the dogs again. Hobo and Cassie were straight down the trail we had just come up earlier. We had a strong signal on Hobo, but Cassie's signal was weak to nonexistent. We could hear Hobo below us now, barking every breath. Our first thought was that he had a bear treed, except no treeing switches were going off. Maybe he was baying the bear? Now he was just to the left of the trail and about fifty feet up the steep incline. We were perplexed. We couldn't see Cassie and still had no signal on her, either.

After a slow ascent, we found Hobo. There was no bear in sight, but there was a hole in the ground that looked like the entrance to a small cave, and he was barking into the opening. On a hunch, we pointed the tracking antenna into the cave and discovered—to our horror—that Cassie was inside. She must have chased another cub into the cave.

The first step, we decided, was to take the other dogs back to the truck, which two of the guys did. Once the dogs were gone, we could hear Cassie stirring down in the cave, to our great relief. I was the smallest among us, but there was no way I could wriggle into the opening. It was much too narrow, twelve inches in diameter at best.

One member of our group, Jim "Grizzly" Gray, lived only a few miles away, so he ran home to get some tools. He brought back a digging bar, a shovel, and a mattock. By now, it was almost dark. We all took turns digging and prying and hacking, trying to make the opening large enough without causing a collapse. The ground was very hard and covered with rocks, some of which were very large, but we were making progress. The entrance to the cave sloped down at a forty-five–degree angle, and we estimated Cassie was about ten feet down. We were hopeful we could get her out, but we also knew that at any moment we could encounter solid rock and be unable to dig any farther.

Six feet down into the cave, we could see Cassie's tail. She was attempting to back out of the cave, but couldn't due to the sharp incline. Rob felt sure he could get at her, so we held on to his ankles as he crawled down into the hole and grabbed Cassie's tail. When Rob tugged on her tail to get her to turn around, she got scared. She whipped around and snapped her teeth, barely missing Rob's fingers, but in a quick motion, he managed to snag her collar. "Pull us out!" he yelled.

Back on solid ground, we checked Cassie out, and incredibly, she didn't appear to have any injuries. It's amazing what a dog will do to get to a bear, I thought. We never saw what she had down in that hole, but it was most likely one of the sow bear's cubs.

Now, I was looking forward to kill season. This would be my second full season because I wasn't counting the three days I hunted the first year. After a good chase season, I knew we were going to have a good year, and I felt certain I would kill my first bear. I had a lot of vacation time to use, so I was out there on the mountain most days. We treed a couple of small cubs that season, but on the one day I couldn't make it, the hunt club killed a bear that weighed two hundred pounds. Bummer.

On the last day of the season, we hunted the Fenwick Mines side of the mountain. We had a good run, and the bear treed a couple of times, but each time, we were unable to get to the tree before the bear climbed down. Now it was getting late, so we rounded up the dogs and decided to call it a day. We rigged Magic and Wahoo on the truck, and Rob and I set out on the five-mile drive from the crossroads on the Fenwick Mines side to the crossroads on Lignite Road.

Halfway across the top of the mountain, the dogs on the rig blew up barking, and we knew we had a hot strike. What the heck, we thought. Let's give the dogs one last chase for the season.

We let Magic off the rig first. She moved away from the truck, barking and walking around in tight circles. Then she lay down and wallowed. I had never seen this before and thought maybe she wanted the smell of the bear all over her. We decided to put her back on the rig, but as I walked over to get her, she took off, barking every breath.

We shrugged our shoulders, then cut Wahoo loose with her. The two dogs sprinted down the south side of Bald Mountain toward the rough road. Since it would be dark in half an hour, we agreed not to let the other dogs loose.

We jumped in the truck and sped across the top of the mountain toward Lignite Road. As we drove, we came to the spot where the rough road cut off to the right. The tracking box told us the dogs had already crossed the road and were heading up Little Mountain, so we floored it out to the hardtop road and hung a right. After about two miles, the beeps got louder, so we pulled over to get a better fix on the dogs.

To our left was Craig Creek, overflowing from all the recent rain. The tracker was telling us the dogs were over there, but we weren't sure which side of the creek they were on. It was dark now. We jumped out of the truck and walked toward the creek with our headlamps on.

Just as we reached the bank, Wahoo came running up to us, soaking wet. A minute or two later, Magic appeared, also drenched. Apparently, they had tried to swim across the swollen creek to get to the bear. This was an extremely fast bear. It had traveled down one mountain, up another, then down to the creek, covering over two miles in less than half an hour.

Unfortunately, we only killed one bear that year. We were happy to have reliable dogs that were showing us bear on a regular basis, but now we had to figure out how to train them to tree only big bears. Still, I felt much better at the end of this season than I had the year before.

CHAPTER 4
My First Bear

In January, Magic came into heat.

Rob and I decided to breed Magic with Wahoo because we thought they would produce some pretty good puppies. So I took Wahoo up to Rob's house and left him there. I asked Rob to take good care of him, and he promised he would.

No sooner had I returned home than Rob called. "I'm taking Wahoo to the emergency vet," he said. "He just got bit by a copperhead."

I hopped back into my truck and headed to the vet's office. Rob met me outside and told me the vet was with Wahoo now. "When I went to put Wahoo in with Magic," he explained, "Wahoo started barking at Magic's dog box. He stuck his nose underneath to sniff around and then whimpered. When I flipped Magic's dog box over, I saw the snake. Killed it right away. That's when I called you." Wahoo, he said, had been bitten on the end of his nose, and his head had swelled up rapidly.

We walked inside, and a few minutes later, the vet brought Wahoo into the waiting room. Oh my gosh, his head was more than twice the normal size.

"He'll be okay, though," the vet assured me.

I breathed a sigh of relief. "Did you give him a snake antidote?" I asked.

"No, I gave him a dose of Benadryl. But he'll do just fine with that. It was a much higher dose than a human would take."

The next morning, there was little swelling left, but Wahoo seemed perfectly normal otherwise. We set him up on another date with Magic, and two months later, they had a litter of puppies. I'd like to say that because they were born with copperhead venom in them, they were all as mean as snakes, but they weren't. All of them would turn out to be excellent bear dogs.

I had the pick of the litter, so I went with a female that was almost the same color as Wahoo. The beautiful, coppery tan color of her fur left me with little choice: I named her Amber.

When we brought Amber home, it was very cold outside. We'd had a big late snow, so we kept Amber in the house for about a month. She loved being inside and was growing like a weed. She loved to crawl up onto my wife's reclining chair and lie on her chest. If Judy wasn't in the room and I was on the couch, she would come over and lie on me instead.

That year, the cold temperatures hung around much longer than usual. But the snow was gone now, so I took Amber outside and tied her up. Well, she wouldn't stop barking—and she had a loud voice. For three days and three nights she barked, wanting back in. When I finally relented and brought her back in, her bark had softened to a squeak. I thought this was a temporary problem, like laryngitis. Unfortunately, those three days of barking had done permanent damage to her vocal cords. The lesson I learned was that while it was no problem to keep a puppy indoors, moving it outdoors had to be done in stages.

We made another trip to Walker Days, a yearly tradition for us at this point. I loved walking around and looking at all the vendors. They also organized night hunts for raccoons and put on dog shows.

But my favorite thing to do was to look at all the dogs, especially the puppies. I found a walker puppy that had come from a great line of hunting dogs and bought her for four hundred dollars. I named her Saber for the markings on her back that resembled a saber sword. Man, that dog loved to eat. Whenever I put a bowl of soft food in front of her, she gobbled it all up. At times she looked like she might pop, and I quickly learned I needed to limit the amount of food I gave her.

In addition to biking, I enjoyed hiking as a way to keep in shape during the off season. I took Wahoo with me on a long hike up the Hoop Hole Trail one day. We hiked up the left side, then took a trail to the right that led to Roaring Run, a stream adorned with magnificent waterfalls. The stream also offered stocked trout fishing, with the upper section classified as trophy fishing. In that section, any fish less than sixteen inches had to be thrown back.

Farther downstream was the Roaring Run Recreational Area and the Roaring Run Furnace, an old iron furnace built out of rock in the early 1800s. I had no idea how those huge rocks were moved and laid in place back then, but it was a beautiful structure. Wahoo and I had enjoyed a full day of hiking by the time we got back to the Hoop Hole Trail parking lot. We were worn out, but the scenery was well worth the hike.

I started taking Wahoo on drives along a national forest road that ran behind Camp Bethel, a Brethren Church camp. Once in the national forest, I would let Wahoo out and he would run behind me to the end of the road and back, which was about eight miles.

One day, Wahoo was running behind me when without warning, he cut to the left and bolted up the mountain. Hearing only an occasional bark made me think he had hit a cold trail, so I sat and listened, but he was very tight lipped. I figured he would get bored and come trotting back shortly. It wasn't unusual for him to go check things out, and then return if he didn't find a track. Well, I sat there and waited for over an hour, hollering for him, but no Wahoo.

My tracking box showed him being about half a mile from me, straight up the mountain. I started the trek in his direction, but even though I had a strong signal, there was no sign of Wahoo. The next thing I saw turned my stomach in knots: a pack of six coyotes, coming straight at me. I had no gun, and all I could think was that these damn coyotes had killed Wahoo. I looked down and spotted two hefty rocks, about the size of baseballs, that I could throw at the coyotes if need be. I figured if Granddad could kill a three hundred-pound bear with a stick, I could kill a coyote with a rock.

I was worried about Wahoo, but I needed to consider my own safety, too, so I headed back to the truck. The coyotes followed me, staying about fifty feet behind me the whole way back. Once safe inside the truck, I put a track on Wahoo, and much to my surprise, the signal was a lot stronger than when I had started up the mountain. I felt much better knowing he was moving about and not dead of a coyote attack. I looked outside the truck. The coyotes were gone.

Five minutes later, Wahoo came walking up. I checked him over and saw no injuries, which meant our adventure had ended well. Still, next time I took him for exercise, I carried my 9mm pistol with me, which was legal because I had a concealed carry permit.

It was now August, and training season was in. We had decided to hunt Stone Coal Gap and were leading the dogs up into an area called Wide Hollow. As we climbed, we got a hot strike, and Magic took off like a scalded rabbit. Then we cut Cassie and Wahoo loose, followed by the rest of the dogs. This was my first year hunting Saber, and I could tell she was going to make a great bear dog.

It wasn't long before all the dogs had crossed the mountain from Botetourt County into Craig County. Gusto was on the road and told us he would drive around to the other side of the mountain. After a long, steep climb, Rob and I reached the top and heard the dogs treeing back to our left and about three-quarters of the way down the mountain. By now, Gusto was around the other side of the mountain, on private property that he had permission to enter. When he caught up with the dogs, he told us they had a sow and her two cubs in the tree. Both of my new puppies, Amber and Saber, were in the pack, no doubt enjoying the experience.

Rob and I sat there listening to the dogs. We had been hunting long enough that we could identify each dog by its bark. We heard Magic, Wahoo, Cassie, and several other dogs. Saber had a distinctive voice that stood out among those of the other dogs at the tree. Just then, she came bounding up to Rob and me, panting. Then she turned around and ran off again, and after a few minutes we heard her back at the tree. She did this at least three times, and mind you, the tree was easily a mile and a half from us. We joked that she wanted us to follow her so we could see this big black thing in the tree. I had never seen a dog run up and down the mountain multiple times like that, but that was Saber's first tree and she was probably excited about it.

During the summer months, we had taken our dogs to a local coon and bear competition. While we were there, we met another bear hunter, Charlie Dunbar, who invited us to hunt with him. He hunted a lot more than we could due to our jobs, and for this reason, he had some phenomenal bear dogs. If it wasn't bear season in Virginia, he would be up in West Virginia hunting or chasing there. He lived near Covington, Virginia, so he usually hunted that area, along with the Pipeline, which was in the vicinity of the Roaring Run Furnace.

During chase season, we joined Charlie and his bear hunting group at the Pipeline. It was an area with only two dirt roads to drive on, so we took one road and Charlie took the other. As we drove, the dogs got a hot strike, so we turned them loose. Over the radio, we told Charlie to listen up because the dogs were heading in his direction. Or at least that's what we thought, not being familiar with the area. Shortly after that, he told us he had cut his own dogs loose and they were headed toward our dogs. His dog Rock, a very fast and gritty bear hound, was the brother of Rob's dog Cassie.

When Charlie's dogs came in from the other road, the bear changed direction and ran straight toward Glen Wilton. Charlie said it was best to drive around to Glen Wilton, go across the bridge, then make a left turn. We should be able to get a track from there, he said.

We went all the way to the gate at the end of the road, where we could hear them treeing. It was a fairly easy walk to get to them, less than half a mile. The dogs had a nice-sized boar, about 250 pounds, up a tree. Some of the dogs were jumping up on the tree while others were just sitting there, looking up and barking. We enjoyed watching the dogs for a while, then put them on leads and brought them back to the truck. It was a good day of chase season, and we enjoyed hunting with Charlie.

During the rest of training season, at times we would hunt with Charlie, and other times by ourselves. I think I saw seven or eight bears that season, the best chase season since I had started hunting with Rob. I was feeling optimistic about kill season and hopeful about finally getting my first bear. I was also excited about having three dogs that were all doing well: Saber, with her powerful and distinctive voice; Amber, sounding like she had a bone stuck in her throat at all times; and Wahoo, whom we still had never witnessed being snippy at a tree.

On opening day, we decided to go over and hunt with Charlie. I was pumped and ready. The weather was frigid to begin with, but the forty-mile-an-hour wind gusts made it unbearable. On top of that, we couldn't even hear the dogs over the howling wind. Not a great day to hunt.

Behind Charlie's house rose an impossibly steep mountain with rugged cliffs that overlooked Interstate 64 near Covington. It made for a tough climb. At times, it felt like we were hiking straight uphill. When we reached the top, Rob and I cut to the left and Charlie went down a finger ridge to the right. It wasn't long before Charlie announced he had cut all his dogs loose. We couldn't track his dogs because their collars were on a different frequency than ours, and after some time, we lost radio contact with him due to the steep terrain. So now, we didn't know which direction to head in, and because we had been sweating on the way up the mountain, we were freezing.

We stood still, trying to hear Charlie's dogs so we could get our own dogs onto the same track. But the whipping wind drowned out any chance we had of hearing them. The cold had really set in, so we went back to Charlie's trailer to warm up. We flipped on the TV and watched as we thawed out. A couple of hours later, the phone in the trailer rang.

Rob answered. "Hello?"

"Rob, it's Charlie. We got a bear bayed in a rock outcrop. Why don't you guys come around to Glen Wilton? When you cross the bridge, turn right until you run into us."

When we pulled up, the dogs were off to the left, barking, and we walked toward them. Charlie told me this was my bear and handed me his .44 Magnum pistol, telling me it would work much better than my rifle because of where the bear was located. We hadn't seen it yet, but Charlie assured me it was a good-sized bear. I headed up to the outcrop, where ten dogs were standing.

Looking for the bear, I peered around to the other side of the rocks. There it was, standing broadside to me about twelve feet away. Charlie recommended I hit behind the bear's ear. I raised the pistol, took careful aim, and pulled the trigger. The bear turned to look at me, then charged straight at me. He was about three feet from me when I managed to squeeze off a second round and jump back behind the rocks.

"He's coming out!" I yelled. My heart felt like it was about to thump right out of my chest. I waited there a few moments, but the bear didn't emerge. I glanced back around the rocks and saw him standing where he had first been. I popped off two more rounds into his chest, and he fell. I had killed my first bear. It was the most exhilarating thing I had ever done, and my heart was pounding like never before. What a rush it was to have a two hundred–pound bear come within a few feet of me at full tilt.

Bear hunting can be dangerous, especially when dealing with an injured bear, and that day I saw why. Maybe I was crazy, but I was glad it happened. It was a feeling I couldn't have imagined until the very moment that bear charged. Now I had a good idea of how my granddad felt when he killed that bear with the stick. The only thing I didn't understand was why the shot behind the ear didn't kill him, unless I had simply missed.

At the check station, they pulled a tooth so they could

age the bear: eighteen years old. Then we hauled the bear over to Rob's to skin and gut it. We hung it from its hind legs, and I skinned from back to front, taking great care so I could see where my bullets had landed. In the chest cavity, I found two holes about two inches apart near the bear's heart. Then, as I skinned up toward the neck and ears, I didn't see a hole where I expected to see one. I had missed the first shot after all.

Being a taxidermist, I was sure to skin the head completely. As I skinned around the right eye, I found the bullet hole where I had shot him point blank. I also found a second bullet hole less than half an inch from the first, beside his right eye.

Using a metal antenna, I probed the holes. They went straight back, missing the skull but hitting the neck muscle. When we gutted the bear, we discovered the bullets had missed the spinal column but did penetrate the chest cavity and hit the lungs. The heart had been destroyed by two bullets when I shot at him broadside. A mystery remained, however: I don't remember the bear turning to face me as I was squeezing off that first shot, yet that must have been the case. Bullet holes don't lie. He must have been looking straight at me for my first two shots. After today's experience, my passion for bear hunting had never been greater.

On Rob's birthday in early December, we started the day rigging across the top of Bald Mountain, then headed down to South Prong, but we didn't get any strikes. So we drove over to the same place we had dragged the bear out the last day of my first year hunting. There, we got a big strike. We cut Magic and Cassie loose first, then Dixie and Wahoo, then Hobo, Saber, and Amber, and finally, all of Fox's dogs. The trail was hot, and it sounded like they had run head-on into the bear at about a hundred yards. Just from listening, we could tell they were fighting this bear on the ground.

The dogs were now moving up the mountain at a brisk pace. It sounded like they had caught the bear again five hundred yards up, on a steep ridge thick with laurel. The treeing switches were going off, so we hiked up toward the dogs. This was going to be Rob's bear. I was pleased to see all three of my dogs at the tree. Amber was barking, but we couldn't hear her because of her damaged vocal cords. Saber, on the other hand, we had heard from the road. Fortunately, she was now staying at trees instead of running back and forth to see us.

Rob shot the bear behind its ear, and it dropped to the ground dead. The dogs sailed in on top of the bear as soon as it had hit the ground, biting it and pulling its fur. It was great training for the new puppies.

In order to legally move the bear, Rob first needed to tag it. He reached into his back pocket, then stopped. "Guys, I have a huge problem," he said. "I forgot my wallet. I'm going to run back to my house to get my licenses." He took off down the mountain.

We sat there for a while, then a couple of us led the dogs back to the truck while the others stayed with the bear and waited for Rob to come back. Later, Rob would remark that killing a two hundred–pound bear was the best birthday present he could have hoped for.

We finished out the season with several more bear sightings and good runs. We also killed a few more bears, which felt great, but nothing would compare to the thrill of my very first bear.

CHAPTER 5
Sasquatch

After a terrific season last year, we loaded up to attend Walker Days. As usual, I enjoyed looking around at the wares on offer. I found automatic dog feeders that could hold twenty-five pounds of dog food and ended up getting four of them. It made taking care of the dogs much easier. I also bought more collars, along with dog leads that had heavy nylon straps to hold on to and chains that dogs couldn't chew through to escape while tied to a tree. These leads also had brass snaps instead of chrome ones, which I appreciated because chrome snaps tended to rust and get stuck after a while. Dog leads had snaps on both ends: one on the nylon strap that attached to a round loop on the chain, allowing you to tie it around a tree, and one at the end of the chain that attached to a collar.

My trick was to have the vendor add two more snaps. That way, I could walk up to three dogs on one lead. I had led as many as ten dogs at a time out of the mountains. Boy, if you hit a track with ten dogs, hang on. You'll just be along for the ride at that point. Whenever that happened, I would wrap the leads around the first tree I found, then cut the dogs loose from there.

My wife fell in love with two beautiful dogs at Walker Days. They weighed about fifteen pounds apiece, and the owner told me they would make good squirrel dogs. I liked squirrel hunting, but I had never hunted squirrels with dogs. Still, we brought home two new dogs that day, which made Judy happy.

Over the summer, Judy and I purchased a boat and spent a lot of time fishing, usually up at Lake Moomaw, near

Covington. It was in Bath County, where my wife was born and raised. The lake had good bass fishing and excellent brown trout fishing. A lot of citation brown trout came from the lake. My biggest catch was a twelve-pound channel catfish.

Judy's mom and two brothers, Eddie and Bud, lived in Bath County. In the fall, I would go deer hunting with her brothers. We hunted with bows, muzzleloaders, and rifles. Some of my greatest hunts were with those guys. One year, they were seeing a lot of bears, including a really big one. But I never saw a bear while I was hunting with them, and it wasn't an area that was great to hunt with dogs anyway, so we never took our dogs up there.

Coming off the mountain one night, I was in the back of Eddie's pickup truck when I heard a squall. I'd heard bobcats before, and this was no bobcat. I was positive it was a mountain lion. My hair stood up straight. Hearing this made me more scared than when that bear had charged at me. The mountain lion was almost certainly up a tree not far off the road, and all I had on me was my bow and arrow. If he wanted to, he could be on me in no time flat. I was terrified the rest of the way off the mountain. I could hardly breathe until we reached the bottom and turned onto the hardtop road.

In the off season, I entered Wahoo, Amber, and Saber in local coonhound shows. These were bench shows, where dogs were placed on benches and made to stand still with their hind legs stretched out a little, backs straight, tails extended and curved up a bit. The judge would look for the dog with the best form, according to how that breed should look. Amber was very talented at this and won many of the bench shows.

Wahoo's strength was the raccoon water race. A coon hide was attached to a pulley on a cable that stretched across a long, narrow pond. Like at a horse race, the loading gates would drop, and the dogs would jump out and swim the length of the pond, about fifty yards. The coon hide would be pulled across the pond, remaining just in front of the hounds as they swam. The first dog to cross the pond scored a point. Then the hide was pulled up into a tree, and the dogs were expected to start treeing and barking. The first dog on the tree got a point, with another point for the first dog that barked while treeing. Wahoo's long legs and massive build made him a powerful swimmer, and he won almost all the races he entered.

One day, I was at a dog show in Christiansburg, forty miles south of us and right off the interstate. Wahoo's trophy case at home was filling up, and for that matter, so was Amber's, from all her bench shows. Looking for another trophy, I entered Wahoo in the water race. He came out of the gate strong, and it was looking like another first-place finish. But then, oh no! Wahoo took his eyes off the coon hide and swam to the edge of the pond, just to his right. He climbed a small fence to get back onto solid ground, then ran to the tree at the end and waited for the hide as it was pulled over his head. Even though he treed first, he was disqualified because he didn't swim the length of the pond. I only entered him in water races two more times, but each time he would just look for the nearest shore. Too clever for his own good, that dog.

Just before the next chase season, a visitor stopped by my taxidermy shop with his dog. He had purchased the dog, Hank, for four hundred dollars after being told he was a straight coonhound. Hank was eight years old, and this man had bought him as a replacement for a coonhound he had just lost. He had only hunted Hank on three nights, and each time he hadn't managed to catch up with Hank until the next day. Hank always treed something, but instead of a masked bandit, it would be a black bear.

This man explained that he wasn't a bear hunter and had no desire to become one. He didn't care for the long chases bears gave. Would I like to give Hank a try in the upcoming chase season? Before I could say yes, he warned me that Hank had bad feet and couldn't run fast, and that, to his knowledge, Hank didn't run deer. I was impressed nonetheless and said I would give Hank a go. The man told me if I was satisfied with Hank, I could buy him for fifty dollars after chase season. With nothing to lose, I went to collect Hank the next day in Montvale, Virginia.

Hank and I were ready to go when chase season started. I decided to use him as my strike dog. We went over to Stone Coal Gap, and I walked my hounds along the base of the mountain on a trail that folks used for horse riding. After a couple of miles, some of my dogs started barking, but Hank didn't, so I moved on, knowing that my dogs sometimes barked on a deer track. After another mile, close to Lee's Gap, the dogs blew up. I cut Hank loose, and he did something I had never seen before: he barked once, walked about ten feet past the track, cocked his left hind leg, and peed for what seemed like two full minutes. He then came back to the track, and off he went.

Hank had a deep voice, but he didn't bark much on the track. I let him run about two hundred yards before I cut Wahoo loose, and in no time at all, Wahoo was out in front of Hank. I then cut Amber and Saber in. I stayed down low on the horse trail and told Rob they were heading up the gap. There were other hunters on top of the mountain who were able to get their dogs in with ours, and together, they treed the bear close to the top of the mountain. Hank, from what I was told, finally joined them thirty minutes later. As time went on, I figured out that Hank could probably tree by himself because he had learned not to bark on the track. That meant he could get closer to the bear before the bear even knew he was there.

That was similar to the way Rob's dog Hobo hunted raccoons. We could always tell whether Hobo had hit a coon or a bear track. With a bear, he would open full cry as he chased. But if it was a coon, he would follow the track and not bark until he treed the coon or caught it. Then he would come back to us, and we could be sure he had caught the raccoon, especially if he had blood on him.

I continued hunting Hank during chase season, and he never barked on anything that wasn't a bear. I was very pleased with him, and there was no doubt in my mind that if I hunted him alone, he would show me some bear. But as a hunt club, that wasn't our style of hunting. There were several hunts where Hank was overtaken by all the dogs, and he would eventually come back to me instead of continuing the hunt.

Hank was slow, but totally straight, and I never knew of a track he started that wasn't a bear. We had a very successful chase season, and at the end of it, I drove over and paid a hundred dollars for Hank. I gave him fifty more than he was asking, simply because Hank was totally worth it.

On the first day of bear season, we went up to Patterson Creek with a new hunter, John. From the dirt road, we rigged until we got to the four-wheeler trails, then parked there and started up Patterson Mountain, just off our left. At the top of the mountain, we cut left and walked about a mile, where we encountered large amounts of bear scat in a white oak flat. We got a hot strike in no time. I let Hank and Wahoo loose, and they went racing down the north side of the mountain.

The north and south sides of a mountain are quite different. The north-facing slope doesn't get as much sun as the south side, so when it snows, the snow stays on the ground much longer. The south slope, by contrast, has sun hitting it throughout the day and usually isn't as lush as the north side.

I heard Wahoo less than two hundred yards from us, and I could tell he was looking at the bear. We cut all our dogs loose. Saber was loud and easy to hear once she got down there. The dogs were now chasing the bear across the mountain, heading in the same direction we were.

The pack stayed just off the north side of the mountain for a little while before all the treeing switches went off. At this point, the dogs were out of earshot, so I pulled out my tracking box. Meanwhile, Rob was approaching from the other end of the mountain. He let his dogs go once he was within hearing distance. We were getting close.

In an instant, the tone of their barking changed, telling me the chase was back on. They were now running the bear straight off the north side of the mountain. About three-quarters of the way down, they turned right and headed back in the same direction they had come from, but now they were much lower on the mountain. John and I headed back the same way we had just come. As we hiked through the white oak flat, we could hear the dogs treeing. With the tracking box, I confirmed they were about a mile below us. John wanted to start down right there, but I couldn't see the ground except for about ten feet in front of us, so I suggested we walk along the mountain until we found a good way down.

Fox was now down on the road, closer to the dogs. The bear was on private land, so he talked to the landowner, Mr. Rock, who gave us permission to kill it. Now, Fox was trying to get to the bear from below while we looked for a safe way off the mountain. We had managed to descend to within half a mile of the tree when Fox told us the bear had jumped down. The chase was back on.

I turned around to look at where we had just come from. "John," I said, "do you remember where it was you wanted to come down the mountain?" He turned around, and we were both staring at a sheer cliff, over two hundred feet tall, at just the spot he had wanted to start down. "We would have killed ourselves." Having hunted the area, I knew the north side to be quite rugged, and if I couldn't see but a few feet in front of me, you'd better believe I was going to be looking for another way. Once you started sliding down these steep slopes, you couldn't stop. Well, technically you'd come to a stop, all right—a very sudden one.

The dogs failed to stop the bear again, so after a little while, we rounded them up and called it a day.

The following week, we hunted Bald Mountain. We headed to the top, in the general area that we had met the last day of my first hunting season. Instead of going off the north side toward South Prong, we went off the south side toward Little Mountain and the rough road. With us were a couple of bear hunters from Augusta County, one of whom we called Black and Tan because he liked to hunt with black-and-tan hounds.

The six of us were leading our dogs down a finger ridge, about a quarter of the way down. That's when it happened: something that would change my life and that all six of us would remember forever. From out of nowhere, and without warning, came this long, *deep, guttural growl/squall*. We didn't just hear it, we *felt* it. My chest was reverberating in the midst of this *deep, guttural growl/squall*. I was in total shock and disbelief. My hair stood up on end. I had never experienced anything like it.

By then, I'd been bear hunting for a few years, and hunting other animals for even longer. I knew every sound that was native to our woods—or so I thought. I knew all the sounds a bear could make: the huffs, the growls, the woofs, and the chomps. I'd even heard jaw popping, a sound that meant the bear was agitated. Sometimes it would happen in trees, but it was even more common when the bear was bayed. I'd heard bobcats, coyotes, and even a mountain lion, the sound that had chilled me to the bone while I was riding in that pickup truck with only a bow and arrow for protection.

Everyone on the ridge with me that day was a seasoned hunter, and we figured we had over 150 years of hunting experience between us. Yet not one of us had ever heard a sound like this before. I glanced at the dogs. Curiously, they weren't barking, nor did they seem the least bit bothered.

"Guys, was that ... a sasquatch?" Gusto said. I was thinking the exact same thing.

For all you non-believers, I'm here to say that sasquatch do exist. Since that day on Bald Mountain, my life has been driven by a singular purpose: to have an actual sasquatch sighting. It's now the number one thing on my bucket list, bumping skydiving (or as I call it, jumping out of a perfectly good airplane) down to number two. I admit I may be a bit crazy by having those as the first two items on my bucket list.

What we heard had shaken each of us to the core, and we couldn't get off the mountain fast enough. But we still wanted to hunt, so we headed over to Little Mountain instead.

We didn't hear a peep from our dogs all the way down to the rough road. But once we made it to the top of Little Mountain and walked a mile to the right, we got a hot track. We cut all the dogs loose, and they raced down the mountain toward Craig Creek. A few minutes later, the tone of the barking changed, and they stopped moving. We could tell they had already treed a bear. We continued along the top of the mountain to the next finger ridge and dropped down to the treed bear. It looked to be of legal size, but small. My guess was between 100 and 125 pounds. We let that one go.

On the subject of sasquatch, let me tell you about my other encounter. Judy and I had just spent a week on vacation in Cherokee, North Carolina. Our drive home on Route 441 took us across the Great Smoky Mountains toward Gatlinburg, Tennessee. It was a beautiful drive we both loved, not least for the plentiful wildlife: sightings of squirrel, deer, bear, and even elk were common.

At the top of the mountain, we crossed over into Tennessee and started down the other side. Minutes later, our senses were assaulted by a dreadful, rancid stench, unlike anything I'd ever smelled before. Hard to describe, but it had a sulfurous odor, almost like a rotten egg mixed with other horrific smells. Our first thought was that a sasquatch was lurking nearby, because we knew people often reported a bad smell when seeing one.

I pulled over and stepped out of the car to look around. As I stood on the edge of the road, a sound came from below, almost like a large animal rustling through the woods. I leaned over and peered down the steep mountain slope. I didn't see anything, but it sounded more like a human walking than an animal on four legs. Whatever it was, it was massive. The unexplained stink along with the sound from below had me convinced this was a sasquatch. I was certain that had I been at this spot thirty seconds earlier, I would have witnessed the hulking beast plodding across the road.

Judy, Landon, and I have been to Gatlinburg several times to attend the Smoky Mountain Bigfoot Conference. At one of the conferences, I met Cliff Barackman, one of the stars of the TV series *Finding Bigfoot*. I spoke with him for a few minutes about my two encounters, and he said yes, it definitely sounded like I had come across sasquatch. All the presenters there were very informative, and I enjoyed them all.

There are conferences all over the country now, and whether you're a believer or not, I encourage you to give one of these conferences a try.

At that same conference, I met a guy who, like me, was a firefighter paramedic. He lived and worked in Gatlinburg. During a break, we swapped stories about our encounters with sasquatch, and one of his stories stuck with me. He had grown up in West Virginia, and he told me that one night, his dad came home late and was pulling his truck into the driveway when he saw that one of their cats was lying in the way. So instead, he parked out front and walked the short distance back to the house. The next morning, his dad sent him to fetch the truck and repark it in front of the house. As soon as he stepped outside, he heard it: a *deep, guttural growl/squall*.

"So, what did I do?" this man said to me. "I mimicked the sound right back." Seconds later, he said, a loud crashing noise came from the area where he'd heard the sound initially.

"Whatever it was, it was coming towards me," he recalled. "So I ran back into the house as fast as I could."

"What's going on?" his mom called from the kitchen.

"Mom," he said, "there's a Bigfoot out there." As he caught his breath, he told her what had happened.

She looked him up and down. "You're full of it," she said. "Everyone knows there's no such thing. Do it again, and this time, let me see."

He didn't want to, but she convinced him to do it. Out on the porch, he made the noise again. And like before, the creature responded with the *deep, guttural growl/squall*. His mom practically knocked him over trying to run back into the house.

As we stood talking at the conference, he imitated the sound for me. Oh my God. It was exactly what I and the others had heard that day on the south side of Bald Mountain. Since then, I have never heard anyone, in person or on TV, who could imitate the sound the way my friend at the conference had.

He told me about his multiple encounters in the

Gatlinburg area, including an actual sighting. I wish I had taken down his contact information because I would love to go on an expedition with him.

At another conference, I met James "Bobo" Faye, another star of *Finding Bigfoot*. He was tall but had lost considerable weight since the last episode of the show. I enjoyed speaking with him. He told me about the time they were shooting an episode at a camp at Mountain Lake, Virginia (which, incidentally, was where the movie *Dirty Dancing* was filmed). Bobo ended up staying at the camp for one more night after his production crew had left, and while he was there, a family of Bigfoot wandered into the camp. I would love to have been there for that.

When I told him about my encounters, he agreed that without a doubt, I had happened upon a Bigfoot. He asked how my dogs had reacted to the *deep, guttural growl/squall* on Bald Mountain. I told him they had paid no attention to it, even though it alarmed all of us hunters. Bobo was not surprised. Some dogs reacted to the sound, he said, while others didn't.

Some of Judy's family members told stories of other encounters. When her uncle worked at the Lower Cascades Golf Course, he said it was common to hear large animals making loud noises in the woods, almost like bears pulling trees out from their roots. Now in all my life, I have never heard of a bear tearing a tree out from its roots.

Judy's brother Eddie recalled sitting and looking out his back door when suddenly a Bigfoot walked across his yard. In another encounter, Eddie saw one at the edge of the woods, squatting and looking around before getting up and shuffling back into the forest. That was just a few miles from where I had had my run-in with the mountain lion.

After our experience with the sasquatch, and as hunting season wore on, we managed to kill a couple of bears. Everything was going well, and then a massive storm system dumped a foot of snow on the mountains.

A snowfall like that can send most of the bears back to

their dens, putting a damper on hunting. While larger boars will stay outside longer to forage for food, many sows and smaller black bears will seek shelter. They don't hibernate, though. It's a common misconception about black bears: while they do go into an extended sleep, it isn't true hibernation.

We didn't let the snow stop us. Back at the four-wheelers parking lot at Patterson Creek, we took the trail to the left of the road like we had earlier in the season. Along with Troy Gussler, one of Rob's longtime hunting buddies, and a couple of other hunters, we trekked all the way to the top of the mountain. There, we headed left toward the white oak flat. We hadn't walked half a mile when we saw the largest animal track any of us had ever seen before, about the size of a gallon paint can. It had to be from a bear that was at least six hundred pounds. But it was a cold track, so the dogs paid no attention to it.

The tracks led straight over the mountain and down toward the road where we were parked. We had Fox drive his truck back along the road to see if the bear had crossed it at some point, but he found no sign of it. That meant the bear must have lain down somewhere between us and the road. We followed the track, and as we got closer to the road, it became clear that the bear had crossed the road. Except instead of walking across, it had used a large culvert to pass underneath.

The dogs still didn't have the scent, so we kept following the tracks in the snow, hoping the trail wasn't any more than a day old. We needed to find where the bear had bedded down. We hiked up and down the finger ridges, through thick laurel and greenbrier. Truly a bear's paradise. Finally, we found its bed. It was still a cold trail, but the dogs were showing some interest, so we cut Magic and Wahoo loose on it.

It was slow going. We kept up with the dogs as they headed in the direction of Glen Wilton, hoping they would warm up the track and we could get the rest of the dogs in on the chase, but it was now late in the day, and we were all getting tired. Trudging through deep snow made it all the more exhausting. Magic and Wahoo were hunting hard, but there just wasn't much scent to go on.

Knowing the bear was still a day in front of us, and that we still had a mile to go to the hardtop road, we decided to pack it in. That was the second hardest day I'd spent in the mountains. I slept very well that night. I was exhausted, but fortunately not to the point that I couldn't sleep.

We finished out bear season despite the deep snow that year. Unfortunately, it seemed the snow had put all the bears to rest by then, and we would find no more fresh tracks that season.

CHAPTER 6

The Split-Up

We found ourselves at Walker Days again, a yearly event we looked forward to. What I enjoyed the most was walking around and looking at all the beautiful puppies and dogs there. I bought a couple of collars and leads, but I also brought home a dog that was a new breed for me: a beautiful, blue-gray Catahoula Leopard Dog named Butter Beans. She was five years old and weighed thirty-five pounds, which was small for a Catahoula, but I was told she bayed bears very well. I took a chance and bought her for a hundred dollars.

I also bred Wahoo to Magic again and asked Rob for two of the puppies from the litter. I named them Cody and Dakota. Rob kept most of the rest of them, including his favorites, Benny and Dozer. They would all turn out to be good dogs.

I had fun training my puppies that summer. They had strong noses and learned quickly how to hunt for their food. Since they would be using their noses that fall and winter to hunt bear, I got them ready by soaking a piece of bear skin in bear scent and placing it in a roll cage. The puppies loved bumping around and rolling across the floor trying to get to the bear skin.

The dog kennels I kept outside had always used the ground as a floor, and the dirt would often get muddy. Not only that, but my neighbors had started to complain about the dogs barking a lot at night, so I decided it was time for an upgrade. I was going to build a brand-new doghouse that all my dogs could live in.

I started in the center of my site and dug the footers.

The finished structure would be sixteen by twenty feet, large enough to house all my dogs. Inside, I made a living area that was four feet wide and divided into eight sections. Each section would house two dogs. In the center of the doghouse, I had room to store food and keep all my tracking equipment. The outer wall had a small opening for the dogs to come in and out of, along with a door I could close to lock them inside at night. Full-size doors inside the doghouse would give me access to the dogs so I could feed and water them. On all but the coldest nights, the warmth of the dogs was enough to keep their water from freezing. At worst, their water would have a thin crust of ice that was easy to break. This was much easier than keeping the water outside. The doghouse even had electricity and running water, which made taking care of the dogs much easier.

Around the outside, I built eight runs, that is, fenced-in areas where the dogs could run and play. I was given three pallets of cement that I used for the floor and footers of the doghouse and dog runs, which saved me a lot of money. All I had to buy was the sand and gravel for the cement. It would have been much less work if I'd had cement delivered in a truck, but much more expensive.

It was a lot of hard work, but Rob and some of the other hunters helped me with the project. In the end, the dogs were happier, I was happier, and my neighbors, who could now sleep soundly at night, may have been the happiest of all.

I saw another Catahoula advertised in the newspaper for a hundred dollars, so I went to check it out. His name was Cree, and he was beautiful: mostly white with a little blue-gray coloration, and very large—over eighty pounds of muscle. I exercised Cree in my backyard, and wow, was he powerful. Every time I stooped down and held my arm out as he ran past, he'd hit my arm and knock me over. The seller told me that the person he had gotten Cree from had another Catahoula for sale, and he gave me his name. He lived in Covington, and I met him at the next dog show I went to there. He had a dog named Bandit with a two-tone, blue-gray hue. He was larger than Butter Beans and smaller than Cree, so I bought him. Now I had three Catahoulas.

During chase season, we hunted the wildlife road just off Stone Coal Gap Road. One day, we were nearing the top of Turkey Trail when we got a strike. We cut Magic loose first, followed by Cassie, Wahoo, Dixie, Benny, and Dozer. They had only run five hundred yards when it sounded like they were looking at the bear. I cut the three Catahoulas loose, and Butter Beans and Bandit took off on the track, while Cree stayed closer to us. They were headed back down toward the truck.

Rob and Fox moved to get in line with where the dogs were coming down so they could cut their dogs in before the others crossed the road. With their dogs in the mix now, the pack turned the bear and raced back up the mountain. They were really putting heat on the bear as they topped out and headed down the other side.

We had almost reached the top of Turkey Trail when we heard the dogs about a quarter of the way down the other side. By the time we cut over to the left and got in line with them, they were halfway down the mountain, and their treeing switches were going off. We had about fifteen dogs on the bear, and they sounded great. I headed toward the tree with Troy Gussler and a couple of the other hunters.

"I'm going to drive around the mountain to get to the dogs," Rob told us over the radio.

"Sounds good, Rob," I said. "The bear in the tree appears to be a cub. No, wait. There's also a sow in the tree."

We were now about two hundred yards from the tree, so we told Rob we were switching our radios off. As we drew closer, more bears appeared. I gaped at the amazing sight before me: a sow bear with three cubs up in the tree. I had seen a sow with two cubs before, but never four bears in one tree. We sat there taking it all in.

Meanwhile, Rob had obtained permission to drive up into a private field, and by the time he parked, he only had to hike up five hundred yards to get to us. With Rob there, we enjoyed the view for a little while longer, then walked the short distance back to the truck. It had been a great day. It wasn't every day you saw four bears in one tree. We treed several bears during training season that year, but nothing else came close to the feeling of seeing those four bears in the tree.

At the start of kill season, we returned to the same spot where we had seen that huge track the year before. We were walking through the white oak flat when we got a strike on a cold trail. The dogs tracked the bear along the mountain as they worked their way down about two miles toward Craig Creek, where Rob was able to get close enough to cut his dogs in with the rest of ours.

Then the trail heated up, and the dogs changed direction and doubled back toward us. It sounded like they were about all the way off the mountain. Grizzly, who was on the other side of Craig Creek, thought they were coming to him. Moments later, he told us they had treed the bear. He could see it across the creek, about four hundred yards from where he was.

"I'm going to swim across the creek," was Grizzly's next transmission.

I raised my binoculars and saw Grizzly's truck parked about a mile away. Grizzly himself was down near the creek, which was heavily swollen from a recent rainstorm. Afraid he was really going to do it, I picked up the radio.

"Grizzly, do not swim the creek," I said. "You won't make it across. The water is too high."

Several more times, he insisted on swimming it.

"No bear is worth someone's life, Grizzly," I pleaded. That's when some of our hunters who were much closer to the bear tried to get to it. Rob and I stayed and watched from our vantage point. Unfortunately, the other hunters couldn't get to the bear before it slid down out of the tree, and the dogs were unable to stop the bear again. But thank goodness Grizzly never swam that river.

An early snow that season kept us from hunting for a few days. But as soon as the roads cleared a little, Rob,

Grizzly, and I headed up to hunt Stone Coal Gap. This time, we did something a little different: Rob and I led the dogs up from the hardtop road, followed a power line all the way to the top of the mountain, then cut right. After four miles, that brought us to Stone Coal Gap Road, near the house of a guy we knew, Frank.

We quickly realized this was a terrible idea. It didn't look too bad from the road, but we had to clamber up and down some extremely steep finger ridges, and there were plenty of blackberry bushes and greenbriers to contend with. The snow was still over a foot deep, even though most of the time we were walking on the hard crust that had formed on top of the snow as it thawed and refroze. We knew there was a trail, not far from here, that went to the top, and now we were wishing we had gone that way.

We finally made it to the top and turned right. Grizzly was waiting at Frank's to track for us. About a quarter mile down the trail, we got a strike on a cold track. We turned Magic loose, and no sooner did she start down a steep holler than she lost control and started sliding downhill. She tried desperately to put on her brakes, but to no avail. It was comical, but concerning at the same time. After about three hundred yards, she was finally able to stop, and she found another way back to the top. We put her back on her lead and continued.

After walking over three more miles, we were getting ready to head off the mountain. We had given it a try, we thought. It was just a bad day. It might even be a bad season due to the early snow, as most of the sows had gone up to their dens. Finding a boar would not be easy.

We told Grizzly we were heading down the mountain to him. But not five hundred yards farther down, at a little rock outcrop with thick pines, we got a hot strike. We turned all six of our dogs loose. We could hear them fighting the bear on the ground, then walking the bear slowly just a few hundred yards off the top of the mountain on the Stone Coal Gap side. Between the dogs' walking the bear and the weather conditions, we knew this was probably a nice-sized boar.

The dogs sounded like they were on the move again, heading up the mountain. Even though Rob hadn't caught up with me yet, I hurried back to the top of the mountain while the dogs stayed off to my right and ahead of me.

Suddenly, the bear crossed the trail about four hundred yards in front of me. Even with my .30-06 rifle, I wouldn't be able to get a shot off. The bear looked to be over four hundred pounds, the biggest one I had ever seen. The dogs stayed with him for a while but couldn't get him stopped, and we didn't see him again.

Later, Rob spoke to Fox and told him about our hunt that day. The hunt was on a Monday, and our next hunt was going to be on Saturday. Well, the next day I got a phone call from Rob. He told me Fox had just accidentally called him instead of Nokie, one of Charlie's friends. During the conversation, he had told Rob, believing him to be Nokie, that they should go to where Rob and Dale had hunted yesterday, because those guys had been onto a large bear but were unable to get it stopped. Rob never revealed to Fox that he was not, in fact, Nokie.

That season, Fox was hunting with us almost every day, and if we weren't hunting, he would go over and hunt with Nokie and Charlie. On occasion, Nokie would come over and hunt with us. So it was easy to see how the lines of communication could get crossed.

Rob was hopping mad as he told me about their conversation. I was upset, too, because I didn't believe it was right to be passing information secretly from one group to another. We were the ones who had put in the effort to find the bear, not Charlie's group.

Rob's plan for Saturday was for all of us to meet in the four-wheelers parking lot at Patterson Creek. Rob had told a few of the other hunters—those he felt would stick with him—about what had happened, but Fox still didn't know he had been speaking with Rob and not Nokie. We planned to reveal this to him just before the hunt so we could hash things out.

Saturday morning arrived. I didn't like the feeling of

the unknown. As a person who didn't like conflict, I hadn't slept well since Rob first called me about the situation. I'd been hunting for several years now with Rob, so my loyalty was definitely with him. But who else would side with Rob on this? I just hoped we would still have a hunting group after today.

Rob and I didn't even put our dogs on the rig at the entrance to Patterson Creek, even though we still had six miles to go along the gravel road to the parking lot. We wanted to handle this matter before we even got a track started.

We pulled into the parking lot. Striker, Grizzly, Soccer Man, Gusto, Troy, and a few others were already there, including Barry Lyle, a close friend of Rob's who had been hunting with him for years. Notably absent was Fox. He probably knew he had screwed up. For a few moments we wondered if he knew something was up and wasn't going to show. Then his truck appeared in the distance as he made his way toward us.

He pulled up and stepped out of his truck. "What's up, boys?"

"I'll tell you what's up," Rob said, not wasting a second. "The other day, when I told you about that big bear we had chased in the snow, I was looking forward to getting everyone together to find this bear. Next thing I know, I get a phone call from you." He pointed at Fox. "You remember the other day when you called Nokie and you were telling him about the bear we had run? Well, guess what, Fox? You were talking to me, not Nokie."

Fox's eyes widened.

"That's right," Rob continued. "I'm not only pissed, Fox, I'm also hurt that you would even think of getting your other group together to kill that bear when it was me and Dale who did the legwork to track it. You know there aren't many bears out right now because of the snow. And you knew me and Dale wouldn't be able to hunt until today, so you tried to get your other group to swoop in and get the bear before we could."

Fox continued looking straight at Rob but said nothing. Rob went on. "I wouldn't have had a problem with this, Fox, if you'd waited until yesterday evening to ask Nokie and Charlie if they wanted to come hunt with us, but you know damn well that what you did was messed up."

Fox seemed embarrassed. He looked down and admitted he had done wrong. After talking about it, we mutually agreed it was best to part ways. Fox got back in his truck and drove off through Patterson Creek to join Nokie and Charlie.

After Fox left, the discussion continued. I spoke first. "Rob, it was you who got me into bear hunting, and I'll always be loyal to you."

Soccer Man cleared his throat. "I've been hunting with Fox a few more years than anyone else here, so I feel like I should stay with him." He paused for a few moments, then looked around at us. "I'm sorry this happened, guys, I really am. What Fox did was wrong, and I understand your decision to split up."

Striker chimed in and echoed Soccer Man's remarks, and said he would go with Fox as well. Gusto said he would also stay with Fox, but added that he, too, was sorry this had to happen. Grizzly announced he was on Rob's side. Troy said that he and Rob had been friends for even longer than they had been hunting together, so he would stay with Rob. Barry said he would stick with Rob because it was Rob who had given him his start in bear hunting.

No one liked that it had come to this, but there didn't seem to be any hard feelings. We stood there talking for about an hour, then Striker, Gusto, and Soccer Man sped off toward Covington to hunt with Fox, Nokie, and Charlie.

It was an emotional day, so the rest of us stuck around to talk a little more. Rob, Grizzly, and I decided to stay on the road while the others took their dogs over to the trails on the opposite side from where we normally hunted. We were hunting the same territory that the huge bear tracks from last season had led to.

As we were talking, Troy came on the radio and told us

they had a strike. He said the dogs were headed back our way. Rob and I wanted to get the rest of the dogs in on the chase, so we drove up the road and parked there, where we could hear the dogs racing up the mountain toward Craig Creek. We were hoping to keep the bear on the side of the creek they were on, but they had already crossed. We dropped the tailgate and turned all of our dogs loose.

At this point, the big split-up from this morning was the furthest thing from our minds. The chase was on, and that was all we cared about. I headed away from Patterson Creek toward Craig Creek to get a track on the dogs, while Rob hiked to the top of the mountain. As soon as I reached Craig Creek, I got a strong signal on Magic and Wahoo. I stopped to listen, and all I heard was an occasional bark. Then I saw Wahoo, who had swum across the creek. Soon after, I also found Magic. Both had swum the creek but apparently had lost the bear.

I got on the radio and told Rob I had both dogs, then I set about tracking the rest of them. This time, the signal was not quite as strong, so I had to think of another way to get closer to the dogs. That's when Rob told me that some of the dogs were now working their way back to the top, toward him. I decided to stay put in case they came back my way, because getting to them would be hard with the creek between us. Eventually, all the dogs came back to Rob, and the ones that didn't we caught up with down on the national forest road.

Unfortunately, this wasn't the season I had hoped for. The early snow had made finding a bear difficult. Then, Fox trying to get Nokie to come over and kill the bear before we could made it harder to trust our fellow hunters. But minus the conflict of the day, we still had fun.

Hunting should be about camaraderie and spending time with friends. Whether you're hunting bear, deer, or squirrel, the sport should be more about enjoying nature and less about the kill. I often think about the day with the four bears in the tree during chase season. That was one of my favorite days in the woods.

CHAPTER 7

Opening Day

Rob hosted a cookout every summer. Usually, I was unable to make it because I worked on weekends. This year, however, I took the day off so I could attend. His cookouts had started out small but had grown as word about them spread. He had always talked about how many people showed up to his cookouts, but when I got there, I was shocked by what I saw. The place was absolutely packed. Rob had set up a bar, hired a band, and as usual, barbecued a whole hog. All the guys I hunted with were there, and I also met a lot of new people. We played horseshoes, had some beers, and ate some delicious barbecue. It was better than working any day.

During the off season, Rob and I took Magic and Wahoo to do some coon hunting one day. As soon as we released the dogs, we got a strike, and they were off on a chase that didn't last long. We followed them to the tree, where they were looking up at two raccoons. We sat there for a few minutes petting up the dogs and watching the raccoons.

Even though it was getting dark, we put the dogs on their leads and started up Wide Hollow. As we hiked up the creek, we hit another track. We cut the dogs loose, but this time they quickly ran out of earshot. Rob thought they had hit a bear. I was excited for my first bear chase at night. The hounds were hammering hard, running up the holler and pulling toward the left ridge. The tracking box was picking up a very weak signal in the direction we had last heard them, but we could tell they were already on the other side of the mountain. The top of the mountain was the county line between Botetourt and Craig Counties, which meant the dogs were now in Craig County.

We climbed the ridge to our left, but it was very steep, and reaching the top took a while. At the top, we stood still for a moment to listen to coyotes howling all around us. They were a good distance from us, but I had never heard so many coyotes at once. We got a track on the dogs, who were now off to our right and a ways down the mountain toward Craig Creek.

We continued tracking the dogs along the mountaintop, and before long, the treeing switches went off. The dogs were still low on the mountain and probably a mile from us. We knew it was going to be a long night.

If we strained to listen, we could hear the dogs treeing below us. We lined up directly above the dogs, then hiked down the finger ridge, which was steep and thick with pines and laurel. Magic and Wahoo sounded awesome, barking every breath.

Approaching the tree, we spotted a small bear up high, then a sow bear came into view just under the cub. It was now one a.m., and we had a long way out, but we stayed under the tree resting and relaxing while we enjoyed the sow and cub in the tree.

We put the dogs on their leads and headed back to the top of the mountain. After a long pull to the top, we cut to the right and started back along the top of the mountain. We hit another track, but this time, we didn't even think about letting a dog loose.

The way out was going to be slightly different than the way we had come in. We got to the saddle in the mountains and used that point to cut down into Wide Hollow. It was much easier than the way we had come up. We still had about two miles to get out of the holler, but it was all downhill, along a trail with no steep parts. We hit two more tracks along that trail. We weren't sure whether they were coon or bear tracks, but it didn't matter. We just wanted to get back to the truck and go home. It had been a great hunt, but we were exhausted.

Later in the season, we got permission to hunt some cornfields. Bears love corn, and cornfields were easy for them to forage. In the evenings, they would sneak into the cornfields and lie down, raking in all the corn within their reach. Then, they would gorge themselves on the ears, move a few feet over, and repeat the process. Whenever our dogs ran a bear out of a cornfield, we found the bear didn't usually run far before scampering up a tree. It was great practice for the new dogs, especially Benny and Dozer, who were really showing promise.

We got a strike one evening, and the dogs ran into the cornfield. A few minutes later, it seemed like they had stopped moving, even though they were barking every breath. As it turned out, they were moving, just very slowly. We had eight dogs on this bear, which we figured was enormous because of its slow pace.

They emerged from the cornfield and walked the bear into the dark woods. We were several hundred yards behind the dogs, who were at full cry and moving at the same speed we were. The tone of their barking changed, which usually meant they had treed the bear, yet no treeing switches were going off. The bear was most likely bayed up on the ground, not treed.

We caught up with the dogs and swept our headlamps over the area. A tree, with a trunk about three feet in diameter, had fallen over with the root ball still attached. The bear sat in the notch where the trunk met the root ball. We trained our lights on the bear, and what a bear it was—easily over 450 pounds. It was also very angry, huffing and chomping and clicking its teeth together. The bear charged the dogs, and they backed away. Some of our dogs were just a few feet from the bear, while others were ten feet back. But once the bear retreated into the notch of the tree, the dogs would close back in on it, with the dogs in front now at the rear, and vice versa.

We needed to get the dogs away from this bruiser, so we put them on their leads as fast as we could. We were working within a few feet of the bear to round up the dogs. We now had five of the dogs, with three to go. Just then, oh no! The bear charged the three dogs that were still loose, and it almost got one of them.

But it didn't return to its spot in the root ball this time. Since there were only three dogs threatening it now, it sensed the opportunity to hurt or kill them. At this point, we had no choice but to turn the other dogs loose again, as there would be protection in numbers. We went through this process about three or four more times. It usually took less than five minutes to round up our dogs with a treed bear, but in this situation, it took us close to an hour. We finally managed to get all the dogs on their leads, and as we turned to leave, the bear saw its chance to escape and ran right past us.

What a night this had been. I went through so many emotions: excitement when we first saw the bear, enjoyment when I realized how big the bear was, compassion for the dogs as we tried to keep them safe, fear and anxiety from being so close to a pissed-off bear, and finally gratitude when we were able to get all the dogs safely away from the bear. I had never felt that much fear for so long since I started bear hunting. But it was time to go home. We led the dogs back out to the trucks and called it a night to remember.

But we weren't done with that bear yet. We would run him out of the cornfields and bay him up several more times before the season was out. Fortunately, we never had as hard of a time rounding up the dogs as we did that first night.

On one occasion, the dogs ran him up a huge tree that was about four feet wide. The bear only climbed up six feet, then walked out onto a thick limb and just stood there. What a sight! After eating all that corn during chase season, he had to be five hundred pounds by now.

The night before hunting season opened, I had to work. But one of the day shift employees had agreed to come in two hours early so I could get off at five a.m. to go hunting. Well, wouldn't you know it: when I got to work, I was assigned to a long-distance transport from Roanoke Memorial Hospital all the way to Wake Medical Hospital in Raleigh, North Carolina. I knew there was no way I'd be off by five in the morning, but I was going to try my best.

All the paperwork was ready when we picked up the patient, so we were on the road in very short order. Knowing I was going hunting in the morning, my partner offered to drive both ways so I could rest on the way back. We made it down to Raleigh as quickly as we could, and I slept in the passenger seat on the way back. Or tried to, anyway. I didn't sleep very well, so I knew I would be tired that day.

We got back at six-thirty, and I headed home to get the dogs. I had already let Rob know I would be late and tired, so I would just stay on the road and track from there. He told me Barry Lyle would be on the road below me.

Barry had been hunting with Rob for a few years before I started. According to Rob, they were hunting on the top of Bald Mountain one day when they hit a track on the Fenwick Mines side of the mountain. When they cut the dogs loose, they sprinted straight down the mountain in the direction of Barbours Creek. Barry hopped in the truck with Rob, and they drove down the mountain to a spot off Barbours Creek Road where they could hear the dogs, who were now treeing. Barry got out and set off toward the tree, while Rob pulled his truck around and found a place to park about three hundred yards away from the tree.

As he walked toward the tree, Rob could hear the dogs barking, but there was also a lot of yelling. Soon, he saw the bear in the tree about fifty feet off the ground. It was dead. A group of hunters stood nearby, shouting. Barry stood about fifty feet away from them with his head hung low.

Rob walked over and asked Barry if he had shot the bear. Yes, Barry said. He had seen the bear in the tree, but a small knoll was blocking his view of the base of the tree, so he couldn't see the dogs or the other hunters. He took aim at the bear's head and pulled the trigger. As soon as the bear fell dead in the fork of the tree, screaming erupted. That was when Barry saw the five hunters and realized he had messed up.

With some trepidation, Rob walked over to the other hunters, who were clearly unhappy. He explained that Barry hadn't been hunting with him very long, and that when he dropped Barry off, neither he nor Barry knew anyone else was there. Since Barry was new to bear hunting, he didn't know he needed to tie up the dogs first. After listening to Rob, the other hunters could see it was a mistake, and together they came up with a plan to get the bear out of the tree.

Now, exhausted after my all-night shift in the ambulance, I entered Stone Coal Gap and hiked to the top of the mountain, where Frank's place was. Barry was below me on the road at the actual Stone Coal Gap. There was a steep slope on either side of that road, which the bears liked because it made it easier to lose the dogs that were chasing them.

Rob and a couple of the other hunters were now coming in from the opposite side of the mountain, near the power line. He said his dogs had hit a cold track and they should be headed toward the steep area of Stone Coal Gap.

Thirty minutes later, Barry said he had just seen a large bear and shot it several times with his .44 Magnum pistol. Not sure if he had hit it, he cut his dogs loose. None of Rob's dogs were with this bear yet, he added. I told him I was on my way down to him.

By the time I got down there, Barry was about fifty yards off the road, saying he had found a trail of blood. I could hear his dogs, who were a little farther down the road and up higher in the steep part of the gap. I hustled down the road to get in line with them so I could climb up to them. Rob and I had always talked about Stone Coal Gap, agreeing it would be next to impossible to climb. Well, I was about to find out if we were right.

The dogs were hammering the bear at full cry. I knew wounded bears could be fierce, meaning Barry's hounds were in a dangerous situation. Barry was climbing up to them from where he had shot the bear, but he had much farther to climb than I did.

I strapped my .30-06 rifle to my back and started climbing. After a few minutes, I could no longer hear the dogs, and I guessed they had moved closer to the top of the mountain.

I kept climbing as fast as I could because the dogs were in great danger against this enormous, injured bear. Then, fifty feet to my left, three of Rob's dogs appeared, coming from the same direction Barry's hounds had.

What happened next took me totally by surprise. The bear darted out from behind a tree, just twenty-five feet uphill from me, and charged Rob's dogs. Blood gushed from the bear's mouth as it ran. I tried to get my rifle off my shoulder, but before I could, the bear had disappeared behind the tree again. I couldn't believe how fast this injured bear was moving. He had charged twenty-five feet out, then back again, in a split second.

My game plan had changed. I realized I would have to climb slowly and methodically to get to where I could see the bear and deliver the kill shot without hitting one of the dogs. I moved slightly right and climbed up to the level of the bear, then waited. When I got a clear shot at his head, I took it.

After I had killed the bear—and I am sorry for this information—I puked my guts out. It was an extremely hard climb, and I had pushed myself so hard to get to this bear to keep him from hurting or killing any of the dogs.

I keyed up the radio to tell Rob the bear was dead, and he asked whose dogs were on it. That was when I realized the three dogs were actually Barry's dogs, not Rob's. It dawned on me that the bear must have whipped Barry's dogs, which was why I had stopped hearing them, and also why they had originally run away from the bear.

I was very lucky and blessed that the dogs showed up when they did, however, because the bear would have charged me instead. I had no idea the bear was still there. I figured since I was no longer hearing the dogs, the bear had already reached the top of the mountain.

Ten minutes later, Barry showed up and congratulated me on my bear. I told him it was his bear because he was the one who first shot it and slowed it down. As we sat there piecing together what had happened with Barry's dogs, Rob came on the radio and told us that his dogs had just treed a sow and cub. They were going to enjoy the view for a few minutes before leading the dogs out.

Barry took his dogs down the mountain, which I was really glad for, because it would not have been fun to take dogs down this steep slope, especially when they started pulling.

After Barry left, I gave the bear a hard shove down the mountain. The animal weighed close to three hundred pounds, but rolling it downhill wasn't too hard. The hardest part was having to pry it free every time it got snagged on a tree.

When I got the bear down the mountain, I ran into another problem just fifteen feet from the truck: the steep bank on the side of the road. To get the bear up, we hooked dog chains together and pulled it up with the truck. Then we loaded it onto the truck. As we headed out, we stopped at the check station so they could look over the bear, then we went to skin it. It was a great first day of bear season.

The next day we hunted was Saturday, and we got a surprise snowstorm. It was only about two to three inches of snow, but at the top of the mountain, it was more like four to five inches. This was ideal bear hunting snow. Since it had just fallen the night before, we knew any tracks we found would be fresh.

At the power line parking lot, we met Troy and his son Shane Gussler, along with two other hunters, Cody Hosey and J.C. Laprade. We rounded up our hounds and set off on the trail to the top of the mountain. It was a good little pull up this trail, but still easier than following the power line up like Rob and I had done before.

No strikes by the time we reached the top, so we cut across the top of the mountain to the west. We walked four miles before we got a strike. The bear track crossed the top of the mountain from the south side and headed north. Benny was standing on his hind legs, just about turning flips wanting off his lead. Dozer had buried his nose in the track. We knew it was a hot track because all of our dogs were barking every breath.

We cut Benny and Dozer loose first, followed by the rest of the dogs. They ran north only a few hundred yards before they caught the bear. The bear turned and headed due west while staying high on the mountain. We could hear them as they crossed the next finger ridge, but only faintly because of the ridge between us. We were now back on top of the mountain, moving west toward them. As we topped the next finger ridge, all the treeing switches went off. The dogs were louder now and sounded awesome. From there, it was an easy hike to get to them.

This was going to be Shane's bear. Troy was at the tree telling Shane where to shoot. He pulled the trigger and hit the bear, but his shot didn't kill it. As the bear came out of the tree, I shot once with my .44 Magnum, and there were a few more shots, but I don't believe any of us touched the bear with our extra shots. The bear bolted straight down the steep slope of the finger ridge and into the holler, where the dogs caught it and started fighting it on the ground.

J.C. led the way off the ridge. I was third behind him and keeping a good pace. That was, until I slipped on the snow, lost my footing, and fell onto my bottom. I slid down the hill a ways, which wasn't a big deal at first, but then my legs went right over a small ledge, sending me into a flip. I came straight down on my head and jammed my neck. My pistol, which I had been carrying, flew out of my hand.

The pain was excruciating, but I managed to stand up and brush myself off. I couldn't see anything. My glasses had flown off, and with 20/200 vision in one eye and 20/400 in the other, I was basically blind. I felt around for my glasses, but they weren't there. My pistol was also nowhere to be found. I did locate my tracking box, but one of the antennas had broken off.

By now, J.C. was down with the bear and had finished it off. I searched around a little more for my gun and glasses but found neither. Boy, I hated leaving that Ruger Redhawk .44 Magnum in the woods. Fortunately, it was stainless steel, not blued, so it would survive until we could come back with a metal detector on Monday. I walked down to meet the group, and some of us led the dogs out while the others dragged the bear down to the wildlife road.

Another day, I was with two other hunters: Rob and J.C.'s dad, White Bear, whose real name was M.A. Laprade. White Bear and I headed up the trail to the left of Frank's house. This was the easiest way to the top of the mountain. Halfway to the top, we got a strike, and it was a hot one. We cut all the dogs loose and they tore out of there, burning it up all the way to the top of the mountain. Once they crossed over the top, we couldn't hear them anymore. Or could we? There was an occasional, but very faint, roar. We continued up the trail, and now we could hear them. They were stopped just two hundred yards down the south face.

The bear was out on a small limb only six feet off the ground, but we knew it wouldn't stay there long. From about seventy-five yards away, White Bear took aim with his .243 rifle and hit the bear's head. The bear fell off the limb and the hounds got to pull some hair. After that, I took the dogs to the truck, while White Bear started dragging the bear uphill. When Rob caught up with him, he helped drag the bear down the trail to the truck.

We treed several more bears that season, but most of the time, we simply enjoyed watching them and let them go on their way.

CHAPTER 8
My Family Life and Vacations

I was the only child of my mom, Irene Joyce Conner Thacker, but my dad, Earl Legar Thacker, had three children by another marriage. I was only close to the youngest of them, Michael Wayne Thacker. My dad was a conductor on the Norfolk and Western Railway, which became the Norfolk Southern Railway. My mom was a stay-at-home mother, and she also cleaned houses for several folks that lived near us.

When I was three years old, we went on a trip to the Great Smoky Mountains. One day, we sat down for a picnic at a roadside table. I was too young to remember any of this, but according to my mom, I saw a bear and took off running toward it. I kept saying I wanted to rub, rub, rub it. My mom told me this story many times. I guess I had a love of bears at an early age.

When I was ten years old, my family got a travel trailer, and we took it on a trip to Florida. I was excited to go camping, but also to visit Disney World, which had just opened that year.

The most memorable ride at Disney World was the Haunted Mansion, but it was at a nearby KOA Campground that my own horror unfolded: While fishing, I spotted a small alligator about three feet long swimming around. Well, I decided it would be cool to catch that alligator. I was using an artificial lure, and I cast my line toward it several times. Without warning, the alligator lunged at my lure. In that split second, I realized this may have been a bad idea. I jerked my fishing pole back as hard as I could to yank the lure out of reach of the alligator, then sprinted back to our camper. That day, I learned that sometimes, what seems like a good idea might not be a good idea at all.

My brother Mike worked for the Norfolk and Western Railway, but he was much more interested in computers. So when IBM offered him a job, he jumped at the chance. He started out in Harrisonburg, Virginia, then got transferred to Montreal, Canada.

One year, we went to visit him in Montreal. I remember seeing the round sphere that was left there from the World Fair in 1967. Mike then took us to a cabin where we spent two nights. We fished while we were there, but the fishing wasn't very good. We only caught one small fish in two days. Normally, I would say any day spent fishing is a good day, but not that time. We happened to visit when the black flies were at their worst, and every inch of us was covered in bites. Dang, did those black flies itch.

Not long after, Mike moved back to Harrisonburg. He only stayed about two years, but it was nice having him an hour's drive away so we could visit. His next move was to Syracuse, New York, and we visited him there, too. While we were in the area, we headed over to Buffalo to see Niagara Falls, then crossed over into Canada to see that side of the Falls. Man, did the U.S. get screwed on their half. Horseshoe Falls in Canada was beautiful, even more so at night when lit up in different colors. We went on the Maiden of the Mist boat ride. It was so much fun being that close to the power of the Falls.

On that same trip, we also visited the National Baseball Hall of Fame and Museum. The Thacker family had always followed the Brooklyn Dodgers before they moved to Los Angeles. That was the day my dad introduced me to shrimp, which he later said was a mistake because of how much I liked them. But they were delicious. Then Mike took us fishing on Oneida Lake in his pontoon boat. The fishing was a little slow, but we did catch some bass, and there were no black flies.

We visited Mike a few more times, mainly on our way to Lake Kipawa in Canada. I loved fishing there. We would slow troll worm rigs to catch walleyes. We caught quite a few, and they were delicious. We also caught some northern pike. One day, my dad caught one about thirty inches long and placed it on his fish stringer. Half an hour later, he decided to take a look at it. As he pulled the stringer up out of the water, the pike lunged at my dad's hand and nipped a couple of fingers with its razor-sharp teeth. My dad didn't want to look at it again until we got back to camp.

Another time, the owner of our lodge told us about a small lake filled with northern pike. I got into a canoe with another guy my age, and we paddled down a small stream to get to the lake. The stream was not much wider than our canoe, and there were a few times we had to get out and pull it. But once we made it to the lake, the fishing was fantastic. The pike were gobbling up the red-and-white daredevil lures we were using. We didn't catch any of the big ones, though. The largest pike we caught was only about thirty inches.

We had some fun times in Canada. Land was dirt cheap back then, so I even thought about buying property and opening a hunting and fishing camp up there. I saw a lot of great deals through a mailing list I had joined.

While in New York, my brother met and married Connie, and they lived there for several years before moving to Lake Gaston in North Carolina, where Mike lived out the rest of his days.

I learned to shoot a gun very early in life. My dad and my uncle Dennis Bowman had me shooting a .22 caliber rifle at a young age. I was a decent shot, so one day when we were down on my granddad's farm, Uncle Dennis asked me if I wanted to shoot his double-barreled, twelve-gauge shotgun. I said yes, of course. I'd been shooting a sixteen-gauge shotgun of my dad's with no problems. Uncle Dennis loaded it for me, handed it to me, and gave me no instructions whatsoever for shooting it. Well, I saw two triggers, so what did I do? I pulled them both. Next thing I knew I was flat on my back, looking up at the sky. I never made that mistake again.

Uncle Dennis and I would also go groundhog hunting a lot, which we both loved. At his age, groundhogs were the only animals he hunted anymore.

I also loved hunting with my dad, who was an excellent squirrel hunter. He helped me get my first squirrel. The squirrel was in a hickory tree, and this was early in the season, so the tree still had all its leaves. The squirrel must have seen us first, because it scurried around to the back side of the tree. My dad told me to keep close watch, then walked around to the other side of the tree and made a little bit of noise to startle the squirrel. When the squirrel popped back to my side of the tree, I took aim with my .410 shotgun and pulled the trigger. That was the first squirrel I ever harvested. I also did some deer hunting with my dad, even though he wasn't a diehard deer hunter. I remember shooting at a couple of deer during our hunts but not killing any.

My dad also loved deep-sea fishing, and we went several times when I was a teenager. On one trip to Fort Lauderdale, Florida, we caught a whole bunch of kingfish. That was a lot of fun. We also hooked two bonitos that weighed at least thirty pounds. Boy, did they fight hard. Unfortunately, we couldn't eat them because they were both full of worms.

On another trip, we set sail in the Florida Keys to catch red snappers and mahi-mahi, also known as dolphinfish, which are very pretty fish with different hues of yellow, green, and blue. When the captain of the boat saw a feeding frenzy happening up ahead, he killed the engine and asked me if I wanted to have some real fun. I was all in for fun, so he pulled out a spinning rod and reel and placed some bait on the hook. Then, he cast into the middle of the feeding frenzy and immediately got a bite. He handed me the pole, and what happened next was a grueling acrobatic dance with this six-foot mahi-mahi I had on the line. The fish was out of the water more than in it. The captain was right: I was having a blast. Unfortunately, the line broke as I was reeling it in. I believe I would be able to land a fish like this today, but back then, I wasn't handling the fish the way I should have with such a light line. What a great day of fishing we had, though.

As soon as I was of age, I joined the Cub Scouts, which

I enjoyed very much. I made all the ranks that I could, then crossed over into the Boy Scouts. That was a lot different. In the Cub Scouts, the leader had a plan, and if you showed up and followed the plan, you would move up through the ranks. But in Boy Scouts, you were in control of how fast or slow you advanced. After I made Life Scout, I only had another two years to make Eagle Scout before my eighteenth birthday. I made it, but just barely.

I loved everything about the Scouts, especially the outdoor activities. I excelled at camping, hiking, fishing, and shooting sports. A year after I got my Rifle Shooting merit badge, I earned my Archery badge. I was able to practice with a compound bow I received as a gift the Christmas before I went to summer camp. When I brought it to camp that summer, I wasn't sure if they would allow me to use it instead of the recurve bows they had at the camp. But they said I could, and I was the first person to qualify on the first day of the process. To qualify, I had to get a certain score using a set number of arrows from thirty, forty, and fifty yards.

On Friday evenings, we had a ceremony called Order of the Arrow (OA). During the ceremony, Scouts who were in the OA would dress up as Indian chiefs and "tap out" new OA members. The chiefs would walk around behind all the Scouts, who were in a circle around a large campfire. When they identified a Scout who had met the qualifications to be in the OA, one of the chiefs grabbed him from behind and held his arms back while another chief in front tapped or smacked each shoulder with cupped hands several times. It hurt a little, but it wasn't terrible. (Due to modern sensitivities, it's now a "call out" instead of a tap out, but it functions the same way.)

To begin the ceremony, three OA members would stand on a hill behind the lake and shoot flaming arrows into the water. What a beautiful sight that was at night. The instructor for the Archery merit badge even asked if he could use my bow for one of the ceremonies. I felt honored to say yes.

When my Aunt Cassie remarried, her new husband, John Paul Lowe, was an exceptional outdoorsman and hunter.

We had a great relationship, almost like father and son. I loved hunting with my dad, but deer hunting wasn't what he excelled at. My Uncle Paul, on the other hand, was the best hunter I had ever known. But he wasn't a horn hunter. He only hunted for meat.

My dad and Uncle Dennis gave me the skills to be a good target shooter, but Uncle Paul taught me how to be a good shot while hunting. One day, he told me we were going shooting, which made me happy. There was a place on my granddad's property that backed up to national forest land, so it was safe to shoot in that direction. But we weren't going to be shooting standard paper targets like I did with my dad and Uncle Dennis, he told me.

When we got over to my granddad's, we climbed up to the back field, where there was a large walnut tree. Uncle Paul picked up one of the many walnuts lying on the ground and said he was going to throw it in the air, and I was to shoot it with my .22 caliber single-shot rifle. Was he crazy? I wondered. There was no way I could do that without a shotgun. Well, he threw a walnut in the air, and I took aim. I missed.

"Concentrate," he told me. "Try to get your sights on the walnut when it's at its highest point and about to come down." I tried several more times, and then: Oh! I finally hit one. It had taken plenty of patience and lots of ammunition, which fortunately was cheap back then. I got to the point where I was hitting nine out of ten of the flying walnuts. I was thinking, man, I'm getting good.

"Okay," he said, "let's change the game." This time, Uncle Paul wasn't going to throw the walnuts, I was. This added a lot more complexity to shooting the walnut out of the air. I tried, and I missed. But again, with more patience, and more ammo, it wasn't long before I was hitting almost all the walnuts I tossed up.

I had the feeling Uncle Paul was going to change the game again, and sure enough, he asked me if I remembered the other day when we had been shooting clay pigeons with the shotgun? I nodded, and he told me to go pick up all of those shotgun shells and bring them over. We often practiced shooting at shells that were sitting on a log, so I thought this would be easy. But no. He threw one up in the air and told me to shoot it. It was a swing and a miss. Because one end of the shotgun shell was made of brass and the other plastic, it wobbled a lot as it moved through the air. He instructed me to shoot just as the shell changed direction, and with a little more patience, and a little more ammo, I was doing well again. I learned faster than I had with the walnuts since I already knew how to shoot. I just had to tweak my technique for the wobble of the shells. Soon, I wasn't waiting for Uncle Paul to tell me what to do. I was just grabbing shells and tossing them up and hitting almost every single one. Now I could hit moving targets without a problem. That made me a hunter, right?

I should have known Uncle Paul had another trick up his sleeve. He pointed at the ground and told me to pick up all the .22 caliber casings we had just used. I instantly knew where this was headed. It was a big enough challenge just to *see* a .22 casing as it sailed through the air, let alone line up my sights on it. It took me longer to succeed at this than it had with the walnuts and the shotgun shells. I got better, but never got to ten out of ten. Eight out of ten was the best I ever did. And when it came time to toss the .22 casings into the air myself, well, let's just say I hit some of them.

It was Uncle Paul who helped me get my first jake turkey. It was the first day of turkey season, and I had to skip school for it (which my mom wasn't thrilled about). He called in three jakes, and I took the one closest to me with a two-inch beard. He also helped me get my first white-tailed doe. It was a long shot from three hundred yards. Uncle Paul was also hunting with me the time I killed that thirteen-point buck when I was sixteen years old.

I remember the day I realized Uncle Paul was the best hunter and shot I'd ever known. I was deer hunting that day, but Uncle Paul was turkey hunting, so he only had his .22 Magnum rifle with him. Suddenly a six-point buck took off running at full speed two hundred yards away. Now, that would be a long shot for a .22 Magnum rifle even if the target were standing still. But from where I was standing on the other side of the buck, I watched as Uncle Paul took aim.

Pew! Uncle Paul fired.

Pew! Another shot.

Pew! Thud. He hit the deer.

I ran over to ask how he had done it. He explained that he was used to his .270 Winchester Model 70 rifle, but with this rifle, he had to figure out—in real time—how far to lead the deer as it moved. He knew how high to hold his gun on the deer, but he had to adjust the lead after each shot. I felt like only a master shooter could do this in three tries. The deer didn't make it sixty yards before Uncle Paul's perfect double-lung and heart shot.

Another of Uncle Paul's amazing feats happened when his brother-in-law Tony made him a bet. Five deer had wandered out to the edge of a field, about five hundred yards away, and Tony bet Uncle Paul a hundred dollars that he couldn't drop all five deer from this distance. You're on, Uncle Paul told him.

Free-handed, he took the first one down as it stood there. Fortunately for Uncle Paul, the other deer didn't run back into the woods but took off in a full-out sprint across the field. Also fortunately, he was using his favorite rifle, the .270 Winchester Model 70. I wouldn't have believed it if I and three others hadn't witnessed it: after five shots, there were five deer on the ground.

Tony handed Uncle Paul a hundred-dollar bill and said he was happy to pay for a performance like that. He told us he didn't think Uncle Paul would even take the bet in the first place, and if he had, he figured Uncle Paul would have no chance of winning because he knew the other animals would take off running after the first shot.

Not long after that, I helped Uncle Paul build a building for another brother-in-law to use for his business. Then I went to work for that brother-in-law, as did Uncle Paul. By this time, Uncle Paul noticed that he was getting short of breath while doing just about anything. It was determined that he had four blockages in his heart, and he was sent to Virginia Commonwealth University Hospital to have quadruple bypass surgery, which he came through. But one hour later, he was rushed back into surgery due to internal bleeding. While in surgery this time, he suffered a stroke. He never regained consciousness, and two days later, he passed away. His death just about killed me. I went hunting that fall, but my heart wasn't in it, and I wasn't sure it ever would be again.

I met Judy Cauley, my future wife, when we were in the same rescue squad together. She was a registered nurse and worked for Roanoke Memorial Hospital in the emergency department. She was also a paramedic. When we met, I was an emergency medical technician, which is the minimum training to be the attendant in charge on the ambulance. Shortly after, I rose through the ranks and became a paramedic as well. I was also a firefighter, and I made it to Fire Instructor I. After becoming a paramedic, I turned to following the emergency medical system side.

Judy and I both took the vertical rescue training and became instructors. I loved working with ropes and learning all I could. I had always been good with ropes and knots from my Boy Scouts experience. Judy taught many emergency medical services classes, and I helped with many of them. She also helped to get the Life-Guard 10 medical helicopter started and flew with them for several years.

Judy's daughter Patty lived in Maine, and we visited often in the summers. Patty had been stationed in Maine in the Navy, then stayed there for many years after she got out of the Navy. One year, as we were driving up Interstate 95, we had just entered Maine when Judy gasped and pointed to a swampy area off to our left. I asked what was wrong. She said she had just seen a ten-foot, maybe even twelve-foot grizzly bear standing on its hind legs. Knowing there were no grizzlies in this part of the country, I said it was probably a black bear, but Judy insisted it was way too big to be a black bear. I couldn't get a look because I was driving, so I turned around at the next exit. She showed me the spot where she had seen the bear, but nothing was there. I truly believe she had seen a sasquatch that day. We both believed in them, but back then, we thought they were only in the Pacific Northwest. This was a few years before my first encounter, and well before the public awareness of sasquatch today.

During another trip to Maine, we were fishing off a boat in Bar Harbor, catching cod as fast as we could reel them in. I was bringing in a nice-sized cod when the first mate of the boat shouted, "Mako! Mako! Mako!" I turned and looked, only to see a twelve-foot mako shark next to our boat, heading right toward me. It snatched the cod I was reeling in and then dove straight down, bending my pole almost in half. As the shark moved away from the boat, I was thinking, please let me turn him. If I can turn him, I may have a chance of landing him. Well, in about five seconds flat, all the line was stripped from my reel and the mako was gone, along with my cod. But what a thrilling five seconds it was.

It was also in Maine that I saw my first moose. We were tearing up I-95 in a Chevy conversion van when a gigantic bull moose appeared right in front of us. It was just strolling across the interstate, in no rush at all. I slammed on the brakes and let him cross in front of me. As he did, I slid down in my seat just to see his antlers because he stood so tall and was so close to the front of the van. We saw several more moose as we got closer to Moosehead Lake.

Before our trip, I had told Judy how much I would love to open a hunting and fishing camp in Canada, and she thought it was a good idea. So we continued driving up to Lake Kipawa so I could show her around and tell her about my plans. But she got a rude awakening when she saw just how remote "remote" could be. Her objections to living up there ranged from the practical (there was no McDonald's within a hundred miles, she pointed out, to which I replied that even so, the lake was full of fish) to the serious (if we needed medical care, how long would it take to get help?) After our visit, I gave up on my idea of a hunting and fishing camp in Canada.

One of our favorite places to take the grandchildren was Disney World. They also enjoyed Marineland and Sea World, mainly for the whales and dolphins. On one trip to Miami, we were staying at a hotel that was right on the water. Judy had classes to attend, so I would walk down to the docks every day with our two grandchildren, Josh and Marina. One day, there was a school of tarpon, some very large, swimming right next to the docks, and we all wished we had fishing poles in our hands. Another day, we saw eight manatees up close from the dock. One of the hotel workers saw us watching them and brought us four heads of lettuce to feed them. As they swam up to us, she suggested we lie on the dock so we could rub their backs. It was a real treat for all of us.

On another trip to Florida, Judy and I hired a guide to take us bass fishing on East Lake Tohopekaliga. We caught a few small largemouth bass and some nice bowfins and gars. Judy hooked into an enormous largemouth bass and reeled it up beside the boat. The guide took out a net that was much too small, more like the size of a trout net. Well, this didn't end well. After trying several times in vain to net the bass, the fish snapped the line and swam off. This bass was easily twelve, maybe thirteen pounds. Honestly, I would have been happy not catching any of the other fish had Judy been able to get that bass into the boat.

The next day, having learned from the guide where to go and the type of bait we needed, we rented a boat so we could give it a try ourselves. We bought some large shiners from the marina, the same ones we used for bait the day before, as well as the same hooks we had used. Like the day before, we took off straight across this large body of water.

All was going well and we were catching bass, bowfins, and gars, when out of nowhere, the weather turned bad. We pulled behind some tall reeds, where the water was calm, to wait out the first little squall. It was short-lived, but the sky looked ominous, so we decided to head back to the marina.

When we ventured out from the protection of the reeds, the whole lake was white capping. I steered into the waves, which were beating the boat to death. We were in a small, twelve-foot wooden boat. Judy wanted to go back behind the reeds. I was sure we would be fine, so I kept going, trying to hug the left side of the shore. The problem was the reeds jutted out well away from the shore, so in effect, we were following the reeds.

At the next little inlet, Judy wanted to find a phone and call the marina. I pulled up to the dock, and a man in his backyard walked down to me and let me use his phone. I called the owner of the boat, and he said the lake could get very treacherous, and we shouldn't have tried to cross it. But he recommended that instead of following the left shoreline, we turn around and go in the opposite direction. It was a circular lake, so he told me I shouldn't have any issues going in that direction.

When I told this to Judy, she wasn't happy and told me to call them back. But I wanted to try at least, so I pulled away from the reeds, made a right, and started going the way the owner had told me to go. We didn't get far. Now, I was as scared as Judy already had been for a while. The waves were crashing over the stern and flooding the boat.

I turned back around and made a beeline for the reeds. I talked to the same guy again, and he told us to tie off to his dock and he would take us back to the marina. I walked into the marina, gave the owner the address of the place where his boat was, and left. Last time I was ever on that lake. If I ever went back, I would get a bigger boat.

We also loved going to Gatlinburg and Pigeon Forge, Tennessee. We stayed at a cabin on one of our trips, and our trash cans got raided by a bear every single night. Naturally, I decided to stay up one night to catch the bear in the act. I stayed up past two a.m. but didn't see a bear. When I woke up later in the morning, sure enough, the trash cans had been raided. Now I was determined. The next morning, I woke up at six and stepped outside. What a sight: a sow with her two cubs, enjoying our trash.

Cherokee, North Carolina, was a real treat as well. I

loved watching elk there. One evening on our last trip there, I counted over a hundred elk. Of those, two were large bulls and several others were smaller bulls. Over the years, the herd there had grown so much.

The Great Smoky Mountains were absolutely gorgeous. I loved hiking the trails, and the waterfalls were splendorous. There were two drives I liked to do whenever I visited, mainly for the purpose of spotting as many bears as I could. The first drive was closer in and didn't take as long. That was Roaring Fork Motor Nature Trail, which started in Gatlinburg. I also loved going to Cades Cove near Townsend. It was an eleven-mile loop, but there were a number of roads that cut across so you could make smaller loops. It wasn't unusual to see several bears while driving the full loop.

On my last trip, I saw about thirty turkeys, many of which were large gobblers. I saw five gobblers together, and the shortest beard among them was ten inches long. I also saw a hen with eight chicks. There was no shortage of deer, with some large bucks as well. I had never seen any coyotes, bobcats, or wild boar there, but I knew they were frequently sighted.

I included this chapter so you could learn about my family—over multiple generations—and see that there is more to my life than just bear hunting. As you can see, even when I'm not hunting, I'm very much an outdoorsman and sportsman.

CHAPTER 9
GPS

During the off season, we looked at some new technologies, including GPS for hunters. Similar to what a person would use in a vehicle, it was a handheld unit that deer hunters could use to mark a stand, blind, or deer scrape. It also had a topographical map that showed ridgelines and valleys.

But when it came to hunting, these units took GPS to a whole new level. The unit could also track our dogs. It displayed a map with an arrow to mark our location on the map, along with the locations of each of the dogs, the name of each dog, and the path each had taken, all in different colors. To do this, the dog collars used radio frequencies to communicate with the handheld unit, which could track up to ten dogs at a time. Our group ended up getting three handheld units and fifteen collars. Then we sat back and waited for chase season to come in.

On opening day, we were ready for the hunt. But since we were unsure about this new technology, we put the old "beep-beep" collars on the dogs as backup. We walked with the dogs until we got our first track, then let them loose on the chase and watched the map as they moved out.

The tracking worked very well when they were up on the ridges, but we noticed that as they made their way in and out of the hollers, we would lose reception. Fortunately, since we were still using the old collars, we could at least tell which direction they were in. The great thing about the GPS unit was that it told us how far away each dog was, rather than just its direction. Distances were displayed in yards up to a thousand yards, then it would start using tenths of a mile. A mile and a half, for example, would show up as *1.5mi*. I knew we were going to love this new technology.

We followed the dogs on the GPS unit, and just as they crossed the top of the mountain, we lost all reception from their collars. Rob was in his truck and said he would drive around to the other side while I continued to climb the mountain with Cody Morris, who had been hunting with us for fifteen years, since the age of sixteen. As we approached the top, Rob told us the dogs were showing treed 0.6 miles from the road. When we topped out, the dogs were to the west of us and 0.8 miles away. We headed west for several hundred yards until we could see on the map that we were on the same finger ridge the dogs were on. They were now showing 900 yards from us.

We quickly learned that the distance shown on the GPS unit could be deceiving. For example, when we saw 900 yards, we thought we would be there in no time. But the actual distance depended on the terrain between us and the dogs, which the GPS didn't account for. On flat land, 900 yards would be 900 yards, but on steep terrain, it could be 1,500 yards, depending on the angle we were walking up or down.

The GPS unit could also tell us if the dogs were barking, and how fast, which helped a lot when we were out of hearing range. Right now, they were barking eighty times a minute. We made it to the tree to find a sow with her cub.

Other than losing the signal from the collars a few times, we liked this new technology. It gave us a much better picture of what the dogs were doing than the old beep-beep collars did.

Later that season, we went back to the cornfields. We saw the big boy a few times, but we also ran several smaller bears. The best part about hunting the cornfields was that most of the bears couldn't run very far after gorging themselves on corn. One night, the dogs were running a different direction than normal out of the cornfield, toward the cement plant on Catawba Road. Cody Hosey told us over the radio he could hear them treed about three hundred yards off the road and was heading over to them. Next thing he said was they were running straight toward him, chasing a black cat. We thought that was strange. We had never seen the dogs run a cat before.

When Rob picked up Cody along the road, Cody was as pale as a ghost. Rob asked what was wrong, and Cody said the dogs had been chasing a huge black panther, and it had run by less than ten yards from him. He managed to catch two of the dogs, but the two others were still running the panther. We knew Cody had seen many a bear up close, so we believed him when he said this was no bear. After the close brush with the panther, Cody was terrified, and I could say I knew the feeling from the time I had heard that mountain lion up in Hot Springs.

During chase season, we learned that although there were still a few issues to work out, the new technology was very helpful. As long as the dogs' collars were within range of the GPS unit, we could see exactly where they were. It was no longer a guessing game. We knew when they were stopped, when they were moving, and the direction they were moving in.

One problem with the old beep-beep collars was that sometimes the signal would bounce off a mountain, making us think the dogs were heading in the opposite direction than they actually were. But with the GPS, if we were picking up the signals, that was where the dogs were. Since it was a topo map, we could also tell how much higher or lower in elevation they were. Knowing how steep the terrain was also helped us to see if we were approaching a cliff, like the time in Patterson Creek, and find our way around it.

Rob's father-in-law, Herman Lee, had been hunting with us a lot. Having gotten on in years, he usually helped us out on the road, stating many times that he could no longer climb hills. Herman grew up around Stone Coal Gap and had forgotten more about these mountains than I'd ever learn. He had been hunting coons, bears, and deer in these mountains all his life. Whenever we got a bear started, he almost always knew exactly where the bear would run.

On the first day of kill season, Cody Hosey, Cody Morris, and I took a couple of their dogs along with Benny, Dozer, Tank, and my Amber and Saber up the mountain. We had already put a cub up the bush earlier, and this was the second run of the day.

At Frank's place, we turned right along the road toward Craig County. About halfway up the mountain, we got a strike. Benny was turning flips, so we cut him and Dozer loose. It was a cold trail that led them up the mountain and to the left, so we followed them, staying within hearing distance. Just before they reached the top of the mountain, the track heated up, and the dogs were sounding a lot better.

We cut the rest of the dogs loose and got them all on the bear. Once we topped the mountain, the GPS was showing the dogs about halfway down the slope and cutting right, or east. I went to my right and followed the top of the mountain to some of the high points so I could see what the dogs were doing. Cody and Cody stayed closer to where we had topped the mountain.

By now, the dogs had run the bear across the top and all the way down onto some private land. They were now turning the bear and running it up and to the west of me. It looked like I was going to be in the driver's seat on this bear. On the GPS, I could see they had treed close to the top of the mountain, about half a mile from me.

It was getting late, and I needed to be out of the mountains soon because I had a meeting to attend that evening. Herman said if I killed the bear and yanked its guts out, they would haul it off the mountain along with any dogs I wasn't able to bring back with me.

I was now closing in on the bear, who was a short distance from me off the north side of the mountain. When I spotted him, he was about a hundred yards off the top of the mountain, in the holler below me and way up the tree. From my position on the peak of a finger ridge, I scrambled down into the saddle of the mountain.

Strapped to my side was my Thompson/Center .30-

06 pistol with a twelve-inch barrel and scope. The precision of this gun was incredible. Resting it on a shooting bench, I once placed a group of three shots that could be covered up by a quarter.

This bear was eighty feet up in a huge poplar tree. I tied up all but two of the dogs as I kept an eye on the bear. He was at least 250 pounds, and probably even larger, considering he looked so big even at that height in the tree. This was about to be my second bear.

As I reached for one of the last two dogs, I looked up and saw the bear hugging the tree. That meant I only had a few seconds before he would slide down. Wasting no time, I got my pistol out, cocked the hammer back, and placed the crosshairs just below his ears for a neck shot. I pulled the trigger. *Click.* Damn, I hadn't loaded a cartridge in my gun like I normally did when I got out of my truck. Well, by the time I loaded my gun, the bear had made the slide, and the two dogs were back on the chase and right on his heels. I cut the other dogs loose and keyed up the radio to let everyone know the chase was back on.

I climbed the short distance back to the top of the mountain and walked back to my truck. I told Rob about how I had pulled the trigger with no cartridge in my pistol. That gave him a laugh, but he said they should be able to get him stopped again. It was only an hour before dark, and I knew I had blown a great opportunity to get this big bear. I had my fingers crossed that someone in our group would be able to get him before the end of the day.

I attended my meeting and called Rob right after. He told me Cody Hosey had killed the bear, and I was very surprised to hear it only weighed 150 pounds. That made me think it wasn't the same bear I had seen. It was possible my bear had crossed paths with the smaller one, and the dogs had continued after the smaller bear. I wished they could be trained to run only big bears. At least we ended up with a bear that day, though.

On Saturday, we decided to hunt up from the power line

parking lot. At the top, we turned left and made our way along the top of the mountain, out past where Shane had killed his bear the previous year. Through six inches of snow, I walked down one of the finger ridges toward Stone Coal Gap. We had hiked several miles and were almost to where the wildlife road turned left off Stone Coal Gap Road. Barry and J.C. had four dogs with them, and I had Benny, Dozer, Amber, and Saber with me.

Our plan was for Barry to go two finger ridges past me, then cut down. To make sure we stayed even with each other, I wouldn't start down the mountain until Barry was in position. Fifteen minutes later, Barry told me he was starting down.

He called me again not five minutes later, and I could hear his dogs going nuts as he spoke. He said he wasn't sure why the dogs were barking because all he could see were deer tracks. I told him I'd be right there to check it out. I climbed the finger ridge back to the top and made my way toward Barry.

As soon as I crossed the next ridge, I heard Barry's dogs at full cry, and as I drew closer, Benny started jumping in the air, almost turning flips. This was all the convincing I needed to cut him and Dozer loose.

Benny tore out of there at full cry, but I didn't hear a peep from Dozer until he topped the next finger ridge. Then he went crazy, and I knew he had found the actual track. He never barked when winding a scent, only on the actual track. J.C. and I turned the rest of the dogs loose as soon as we heard Dozer. I asked J.C. where Barry was, and he said he had walked down between the two finger ridges looking for the track.

A few minutes later, Barry came back up. "I don't think this is right," he said. "I've been all over down in that holler looking for the track. I see plenty of deer tracks, but no bear tracks."

I told him that when Benny turned flips, that meant he had scented a bear. I had come to trust Benny and knew that when he was pulling and barking, but not turning flips, it was probably a deer he was after. But the flips always meant a bear. Benny had never lied about that.

Dozer wasn't a dog that opened on a bear that he was only winding. He only opened when he had his nose in an actual track. That was why I had waited until I got confirmation from Dozer before turning the other dogs loose. Benny's nose was what we called a warm nose, meaning if the track was too old, he wouldn't be able to smell it. Dozer, on the other hand, had a cold nose, so even on a much older track, he could still sniff out the trail.

And the two dogs hunting together was a sight to behold. On a hot trail, Benny would take off leading, with Dozer keeping pace. But on a cold track, Dozer would cold trail while Benny followed, waiting for the trail to warm up.

"Just watch," I told Barry. "The bear tracks will be over on the next finger ridge."

"I hope you're right about that," he said. "But I have my doubts."

Well, it wasn't long before the dogs treed two finger ridges over. From down on the wildlife road, J.C.'s dad, White Bear, said he could hear the dogs up the mountain from him and that he was sending the shooter up now. Cutting over two finger ridges took a while due to the steepness of the terrain, but when we got there, we found a 250-pound bear sitting in a notch in the tree, fifty feet up. The tree was about ten feet up the other side of the V holler from where we were.

We sat there waiting for the shooter, who was still on his way up. After half an hour, White Bear came on the radio and warned us that another group of hunters was headed our way. Right now, they were on top of the mountain with their dogs loose, so we would need to take care of business as soon as possible.

When the shooter arrived, we gave him five minutes to rest. As soon as he was ready, we told him to shoot between the eyes because of the way the bear was facing us. He lined up the shot and pulled the trigger of his 7mm rifle. The bear fell, but immediately got its head caught in a fork of the tree. We now had a bear stuck fifty feet up. The trunk of the tree was almost two feet in diameter at the ground and had no limbs below the fork where the bear was lodged.

We hatched a plan. We called Rob at work and asked him to bring his climbing tree stand to us. By now, two of the dogs from the top of the mountain had shown up, but we didn't attempt to place them on leads. We knew the other hunters were probably not going to see this scenario for what it was, and tying up their dogs would only make things worse, so we just let them stand and tree on the dead bear.

Thirty minutes went by, then forty, and still no Rob. A few more dogs had shown up in the meantime, and now there were eight dogs from the other group at the tree.

Three hunters showed up just then and immediately accused us of killing *their* bear that *they* had started on top of the mountain. It did no good to tell them that we had started the track two ridges over, and not only that, but none of their dogs were even at the tree when we killed the bear.

"Enjoy your trophy," one of the hunters scoffed as he walked off. Then he turned around and pointed up at the bear. "That's exactly where the bear is going to be at this time next year, too. By the way, don't even think about cutting that tree down. We'll be out on the road listening for chainsaws."

As we waited for Rob, I pieced together what had happened. Their dogs must have heard our dogs and started barking, which was why they cut their dogs loose. But I think they honestly believed their dogs had picked up the track first.

Two hours after we had killed the bear, Rob showed up with his climbing tree stand. Right away we hit a snag: it wouldn't fit around the base of the tree. We had the shooter get on our shoulders, and he managed to get it around the tree, but it was tight fit. Before he started climbing, we tied a large limb to the tree stand so he could use it to force the bear's head free. But when he reached the bear, he was unable to budge it. The problem was he was trying to pry up 250 pounds of bear while standing on a climbing tree stand rated at three hundred pounds while he was fifty feet in the air. We needed a new plan.

The tree was situated about ten feet up a steep slope. The holler itself was V-shaped, so our plan was to tie all the dog leads together, throw them up to the shooter and have him tie them around the bear's neck. Then we would climb up the opposite slope until we were almost level with the bear, and pull.

After a few tosses, the shooter caught the leads. He tied one end around the bear's neck and dropped the other end down to us. The five of us on the ground took the leads and climbed up the opposite ridge. We pulled on the leads with all our might while the shooter tried to pry the bear's head out of the notch with the stick. *Snap!* Our makeshift chain broke apart, and we all fell to the ground. The bear hadn't moved an inch.

We reattached and tried this three more times, each time falling to the ground. We were starting to think the hunter from the other group was right, that the bear would still be hanging there a year from now. But we took a few minutes to summon our strength, then gave it one more try. The bear fell. What a wonderful feeling to see that bear lying on the ground at last. We dragged the bear down to the truck and called it an amazing day hunting.

Barry came up to me and said he really thought it had been a deer because he didn't see any tracks. I told him I had never seen Benny turning flips like that when it wasn't a bear. He swore he would never question Benny again, especially when he was turning flips.

The next week, J.C. and I decided to hunt by ourselves. We went up from the power line parking lot and turned left at the top. We hadn't gone far before Benny was again turning his flips and Dozer was barking every breath, telling us the bear had crossed the top. There was still snow on the ground, but we couldn't see any tracks because as the snow had thawed and refrozen, it left a hard crust on the ground.

The dogs were all pulling to the right, in the direction of Stone Coal Gap Road. We cut all the dogs loose and they tore out of there, sounding awesome. It was a hot track if I'd ever seen one. We watched until they were well over halfway off the mountain, then headed back to our trucks and drove toward Stone Coal Gap. We knew going in it would be hard with just the two of us hunting and no one on the road. To get from the top of the mountain to the point where the bear and dogs had come off the mountain would take well over an hour.

We drove slowly, watching the GPS to see how well the tracks on the screen matched up with the actual tracks. We stopped right on the tracks the GPS was showing us, but the snow was crusted over so we couldn't see the actual tracks. Just to our left, there was a creek, and we could see where the bear had smashed through the ice. We then knew the tracks matched.

We had no GPS signal on them from here, so we hauled out the old tracking box. We picked up a faint beep across the next mountain, which meant they were now in Craig County. Across that mountain lay a vast swath of land called Little Cuba. This was an area we hated tracking and hunting in because it was notorious for loss of signal due to the many steep, rolling hills.

We kept driving out of Broad Run and turned right when we hit the hardtop. That took us to New Castle, where we could access Little Cuba. Usually, the hardtop road was a good place to get a signal, but this time we had no signal from either the GPS or the beep-beep collars.

We turned onto Craig Creek Road, toward the base of Bald Mountain. Now we had a new issue: we were picking up a faint beeping, but we weren't certain of the direction it was coming from. It was slightly stronger toward Bald Mountain, but it was hard to tell whether that was the real signal or a bounced signal. We decided to ask for Rob's help. He was at work when we called but said he would be there as soon as possible.

While we waited for Rob to show up, we ventured part of the way up Bald Mountain, where we detected a strong beep-beep signal from Little Cuba, but still no GPS signal. It had now been almost six hours since we had cut the dogs loose.

As we drove back down the mountain, Rob came on the radio and informed us that he was now on top of the mountain and had a GPS location on the dogs. They were showing treed in Little Cuba, over toward the bar, a hinged gate that blocked the road.

Rob met us as we entered Little Cuba. By that time, we were picking up the dogs on our GPS unit, but they were no longer showing treed. When we arrived at the bar gate, we sat and waited for the dogs to show up. Soon, they were just 0.5 miles away and heading toward us, but we could not hear any barking, and none of the bark meters were going off.

Rob let us know we had messed up, which we both already knew. He said it was too long of a haul making it all the way to Bald Mountain. One of us should have climbed the mountain to where the dogs had crossed Stone Coal Gap Road. That way, we would have had a GPS location on the dogs. Meanwhile, the other one of us could have gone into Little Cuba, and maybe we would have been able to get a better location on the dogs. If not, at least the person on top of the mountain would have known where the dogs were. This was a good learning experience for us as we got familiar with all the new technology.

With a huge snowstorm in the forecast, we knew next weekend would be our last chance to hunt for the season. I really wanted to get back on that bear I hadn't killed when I forgot to load my gun. If I couldn't redeem myself, I was never going to live that down.

That weekend, we headed back up to Frank's the same way we had on opening day. On our way up the mountain, we got a strike in the same place we had last time. Benny started doing his flip thing, so we cut all the dogs loose and the chase was on.

They ran the bear off the mountain in almost the same direction as last time, but this time when they were halfway off the mountain, they cut hard to the right and didn't climb back up. Instead, they went two or three miles along the mountain.

From the top, we tried to stay with them as long as we could.

The sky grew overcast as the clouds rolled in, and we knew we didn't have much time. By now, the dogs had split up, with some tracking back in the direction they had come from, and others cutting down the mountain. We were able to round up all the dogs that were backtracking and bring them to the trucks, then start the nearly forty minute drive to the other side of the mountain. When we got there, the four dogs that were still loose were 0.7 miles away, and they appeared to be following a dirt trail near where we had parked. Rob and I started up the trail, and in less than ten minutes we had all of them. No sooner had we snapped on the dog leads than the first snowflake fell.

By the time we got back to the truck, we could see our tracks in the snow. There were already three inches of snow on the ground after we had dropped everyone off at their own vehicles. When I arrived home forty-five minutes later, six inches had fallen in whiteout conditions. It wasn't supposed to stop snowing until tomorrow evening. This was going to be a huge storm.

The next morning, I woke up to over two feet of snow. It was no longer a whiteout, but it was still coming down steadily. When it finally stopped just before nightfall, we were buried under thirty inches of snow. Without a doubt, it was a season-ending snowfall.

It had still been a great season, even though it was cut short by two weeks. We had killed four or five bears, let several smaller bears go so we could run them again another day, and seen a number of sows with their cubs up in trees, a sight that never got old.

CHAPTER 10
Five in a Tree

After a fruitful but shortened season last year, and with the new GPS technology under our belts, we were excited to get chase season started. Cody Morris was the first to arrive that morning. He told us that as he was driving up Stone Coal Gap, he had run across a 150-pound bear in the middle of the road. This bear was in no hurry, he said, and once it wandered off the road, it just sat back on its haunches for a few minutes, then shuffled off into the woods. Rob and I were just a few minutes behind him, so he said he would wait until we got there before running the track.

When we arrived, Cody showed us where the bear had been. Rob dropped his tailgate, and his new dogs, Maybell and Reno, hit the track. Within moments, all of Rob's dogs were on the track full cry. Cody and I dropped our tailgates, too, and the chase was on. At first, the dogs stayed low on the mountain. They had only run a short distance before they cut lower on the mountain and turned back toward Stone Coal Gap Road. Seeing they were about to run onto private land, Cody raced over to stop them but was only able to catch one of the dogs. The rest of them ran across the dirt road, heading in the direction of a hardtop road.

Cody and Rob drove over to where the dogs would cross the hardtop. I hung back on Stone Coal Gap Road to catch the last dog that hadn't joined the rest of the pack. Somehow, this chase had taken a wrong turn, and we couldn't picture the path the bear had taken. Rob and Cody intercepted the dogs as they approached the road and managed to catch them all, while I caught the one dog left behind.

Since Cody had seen the bear in the road earlier, we

thought it would be an easy run on a hot track. But even though it hadn't gone as planned, we weren't giving up. We drove along Stone Coal Gap Road to an area we called The Bowl. After spending time as a guide in Maine, Rob had brought back a few new techniques that changed the way we hunted. Now, we just pulled up to a trail and dropped the tailgate. That way, the dogs would take off up the trail without us having to walk them.

The dogs had made it 1.2 miles to the top of the mountain and hadn't hit a track yet. Well, after trying for a couple of hours, most of the dogs were now on their way back to us. Maybell and Reno, on the other hand, said no, it was too early to call it a day, and continued walking the top of the mountain toward Frank's place. That was a four-mile walk from where we were.

Cody was already around at the Botetourt County Dump. He had headed over there when the dogs first crossed the top of the mountain. I was staying up with Maybell and Reno, driving back the way we had come in. When I got to Frank's, the dogs were now 0.9 miles from me, and I could hear them barking for a moment before they crossed over the top of the mountain.

By now, Rob had rounded up all the other dogs and was headed toward Frank's. Because I was off the south side, I needed to reposition in order to track better, so I set off driving toward Roaring Run Furnace. As I headed down the mountain, Cody came on the radio and said he thought they had the bear. Both Reno and Maybell were now showing treed. When I pulled up to the furnace, the dogs were 0.9 miles away, and I could make out an occasional, faint bark. Cody reported his position as 1.2 miles from them.

Rob and Cody came to the furnace, where Rob's daughter's boyfriend, Little, had also joined our group. Little and I started the climb to the dogs. It was hot, and the dogs had been hunting for several hours now, so we knew they were tired. We figured that was why they were not barking a lot under the tree. But when we got to within three hundred yards of them, they were no longer showing treed.

Seeing them start up the mountain, we called to them. Luckily, they came back to us and we headed for the truck. The dogs had had two good runs, but unfortunately, we didn't get to see a bear. Well, Rob, Little, and I didn't. Cody cheated and saw one before the hunt had even started.

Later that chase season, Cody Hosey gained access to some cornfields on the Craig Creek side of Patterson Mountain, which we were very excited about. Bears love to eat corn, and it fattens them up. That's why it was almost always a matter of when, not if, we would get a strike when hunting the cornfields.

This time, we were only given permission to take one truck in, which limited us to a couple of hunters plus the dogs. So Hosey and one other hunter would go in on the Craig Creek side of the mountain and around the edges of the field, trying to get a hot strike, while the other hunters would take their dogs from Patterson Creek to the top of the mountain. From there, they would join their dogs with the hounds that had hit the track in the cornfields.

Cody Morris and I took Reno, Maybell, Puppy, Forrest, Queen, and a few more dogs and headed to the top of Patterson Mountain. Hosey was waiting for us to get close to the top before taking his five dogs along the edge of the cornfields to get a bear started. But before we reached the top of the mountain, we got a hot strike and cut all the dogs loose. We let Hosey know, and he said he would get a second chase started once he got a strike, which happened a few minutes later.

Our dogs were at full cry and picking up speed as they topped the mountain, heading due east. They looked to be only about a hundred yards off the north side, but being on top, we could hear both packs of hounds. Hosey's dogs had now come close to halfway up the mountain, and they were sounding awesome. Our own pack was now over a mile from us.

Now that we had the second generation of GPS, called Alpha 100, we weren't losing the dogs as often as we used to.

There were still dead spots in some of the deep hollers, but range and reception were much improved.

Morris and I had trekked a mile or so across the top of the mountain when Hosey announced his dogs were treed. Our dogs were now 0.8 miles from us and about halfway off the north side. They were still moving but more slowly than before.

As we sat on top of the mountain for a little bit, we could hear our dogs at full cry. I believed they were about to tree this bear. We could also faintly hear Hosey's pack, and it wasn't long before Hosey told us he had a 200-pound sow with a 50-pound cub about forty feet up in the tree. Our dogs, who were still halfway off the north side and in front of us, had just pulled up treed. We continued across the top of the mountain until we were on the same ridgeline as the dogs, then cut down to the tree.

Wow, what a beautiful sight: a sow, about 175 pounds, with two second-year cubs that by kill season would meet the 100-pound live weight requirement. That was the minimum size to kill a bear in Virginia. However, our group always made sure the bears we killed were 150 pounds or larger, otherwise we would let them live for another chase. What a wonderful morning. It wasn't yet noon, and our group had already seen five bears.

As I got older, I no longer wanted to kill bears just because they were legal. The real work started when you pulled the trigger, because dragging a bear out of these steep and thick mountains wasn't easy. I got a lot more joy out of treeing the bears, then sitting and watching them up in the tree while our dogs did what they were bred to do. They loved the chase as much as I did.

Between hunting in Patterson Creek and Stone Coal Gap, we had many more great hunts during chase season, and we were looking forward to kill season. Reno and Maybell were doing very well, as were Tank, Puppy, and Forrest, our other great hounds.

On the first day of kill season, we decided to hunt up

in Wide Hollow. Upon reaching the first saddle, we cut to the right and headed up the very steep, thick ridge. As we topped out, we got a strike, and Reno and Maybell set about cold trailing down the ridge in the direction of the horse trail. We could barely hear them after several minutes, but it sounded like the track was heating up, so we cut the dogs loose, and they all raced to catch up with Reno and Maybell.

The dogs were now 0.9 miles from us and cutting to the east as they headed into Lee's Gap, which was very much bear country. The terrain was steep, with many finger ridges thick with pine trees and mountain laurel. The dogs had picked up the pace. They were now moving away from us along the mountain, just starting to climb. We knew it would be a long way to get to where the dogs were headed. We had to come back down the ridge we were on, but once we got back to the saddle, it would be easy going for the next two miles.

The path we had come up in Wide Hollow had turned into a dirt road. It had some growth on it, but at least there were no big hills to wear us out. On this road, which continued all the way through to Price Mountain Road, there were two saddles: the one we were at now and another about two miles away. These two saddles were the best access points to the top of the high knolls on each side of Lee's Gap. When we finally reached the second saddle, we had no GPS signal and only a very faint beeping on the dogs.

From down at the gate on Price Mountain Road, Rob told us the dogs were high on the mountain and still moving in the direction of Kelly Hollow. They were about two miles from the hardtop road, which they would need to cross in order to get to Kelly Hollow. So, we began the climb to the top of the second high knoll. Once we were on top, there would only be some small peaks to climb, and we would definitely have some laurel to trudge through, but for the most part, it would be easy walking.

Once we topped out, we were still unable to get a GPS signal, but the beep-beep signal had improved slightly. We advised Rob that we were on top and were going to take a five-minute break, then continue across the top of the mountain. He said he couldn't hear the dogs, but the bark meters were going off at sixty barks a minute. According to Rob, they were just off the top of the mountain on the south side. That was the opposite side of the mountain from where Rob was. For us, it was off to our right.

We made it a couple of peaks over, and the GPS now showed the dogs about two miles in front of us. We were just hoping they stayed on this mountain and didn't cross over into Kelly Hollow, because then we could just walk the dirt road out, which would be much easier.

Just then, Rob told us the dogs had treed on the last peak before cutting down the mountain to Kelly Hollow. We were excited to hear this. The twelve-year-old shooter was with him in the truck, and he said they were going to find a parking spot at the base of the mountain and hike up together. I didn't envy the hike they had ahead of them. Even though their hike was a shorter distance than ours, it was a very steep, rocky climb, thick with laurel.

In the tree was a 175-pound boar bear. We sat there watching the bear, which was sitting on a limb fifteen feet up. I also enjoyed watching the hounds as they stood jumping and clawing at the base of the tree, trying to climb up to the bear. With a running start, the dogs could get almost eight feet up the tree before losing momentum.

Thirty minutes later, Rob showed up with the shooter, who was seeing a bear in the wild for the very first time. He was so excited. He said he loved how the dogs were so loud, he couldn't hear anything else. We let him calm down and enjoy the sight of the bear and the sound of the dogs for about ten minutes, then we put all the dogs on leads and tied them up about fifteen feet from the tree. We positioned the dogs around the tree so the bear wouldn't have an escape route.

The shooter took aim at the side of the bear's head and pulled the trigger. The bear tumbled out of the tree, but it was far from dead. Even though the shot had hit the bear's head, it wasn't a perfectly placed shot. We knew our dogs risked being injured or killed running after a wounded bear, but after seeing the heavy trail of blood the bear was leaving behind, we knew he wouldn't make it very far.

We cut the dogs loose, and the chase was back on. They raced off toward the gate on Price Mountain Road, and we moved in that direction behind them. The dogs were running at full speed, and they weren't slowing down. We were surprised at how fast this bear was running despite having lost so much blood. The bear had already run for over a mile and was still going strong.

The dogs were now low in the holler and still moving in the direction of the gate. We knew our best bet was to drive over to the gate in Rob's truck. As we wound our way up the mountain, our indicator showed the dogs treed. We followed Price Mountain Road, and when we got to the gate that opened onto the dirt road we were on earlier, another road split off and went down the hill, where it dead-ended after half a mile. Just before that, and seventy-five yards off the road to our left was where the dogs were showing treed. We walked down.

The bear was in the tree, but it was wobbly now and had blood dripping from its head. The tree was covered in blood. We had no idea how this bear was still alive, but our twelve-year-old shooter put the finishing shot in its head, and the bear fell out of the tree and hit the ground dead.

This time, we had backed him up with another rifle, but the shooter's second shot was perfectly placed. We were baffled at how much blood this bear had lost and how it had run the distance it had. We checked over all the dogs to make sure they were okay. Most were covered in blood, but none were injured. In a way, it was better we didn't kill the bear the first time, because from where we were now, we only had a seventy-five–yard drag to the truck along a slight incline.

The next Saturday, we were back at the same cornfields we had hunted during chase season. The plan was to take the dogs up from the cornfields as we had done before. The difference this time was that the cornfields had been cut and there was no standing corn, so we wouldn't be running any bears out. While Cody Hosey and Barry took their dogs up, we drove along the hardtop road, since last time all five bears had treed on the Craig Creek side of the mountain.

As we drove, the dogs hit a cold track, so we let Reno and Maybell loose to follow the track up the mountain to the west. They were at full cry just prior to topping out, so Cody let his dogs out to join up with them. I headed over to Patterson Creek Road to track from there.

When I arrived, several other trucks from another bear hunting group were parked there. Some of the hunters were in their trucks, but most appeared to be hiking up the mountain to the right side of the road.

When I got in line with the dogs, they were now 0.8 miles from me and showing treed. All our dogs were to the left of the road, but I could hear other dogs to the right. From the top of the mountain, Cody and Barry said they were nine hundred yards from the dogs now. Since they were closer to the dogs and also walking downhill, I knew they would get to the tree before me.

Sure enough, after a few minutes, they said they were turning off their radio. I kept mine on, and five minutes later, it crackled back to life with Cody's voice: "Uh, we have five dogs in a tree," he said, "and they're fifty feet in the air."

I thought I had heard wrong, so I keyed up. "Did you say you have five *bears* in the tree?"

"Negative," Cody replied. "We got five *dogs* in the tree—repeat, five dogs—and they are at least fifty feet in the air."

I was totally confused, but I continued climbing so I could see for myself. Suddenly, my three dogs cut to my left and charged back down the mountain, full cry, toward my truck. There was a pack of dogs on the opposite mountain, and they sounded treed, so that was probably where my dogs were going. In the meantime, Rob had parked his truck and was heading up, about three hundred yards behind me.

As I approached the tree, I was baffled by the sight before me. Three dogs were fifty feet up in the tree, with another about twenty feet up, who just then lost his footing and fell out of the tree. Cody and Barry ran over to him and were relieved when he stood up. He appeared to be okay. I continued toward the tree. The mountain was very steep but fortunately, there wasn't much underbrush, and I could see and hear a long distance.

The dogs were in a poplar tree, about twenty inches wide at the base, that had blown over and was lying at a sixty-degree angle against another poplar tree. Barry told me there were five dogs up in the tree when they had arrived, and the first one had fallen from about thirty feet up when it tried to back down. He said the two dogs that had fallen looked okay with no injuries.

Now, Cody was straddling the tree, almost like he was riding a horse, climbing up to get to the remaining three dogs. Barry and I watched, speculating about how the dogs had ended up in this situation. The only plausible way this could have happened, we figured, was that the bear had climbed the leaning tree, leaving his scent as he climbed. Then, he slid down the other tree at the point where the two trees met.

Rob showed up and checked the two dogs that had fallen, and agreed they were uninjured. Cody was now about twenty feet up, coaxing the remaining dogs out of the tree. One of them was almost within arm's reach of Cody when it slipped and fell about twenty-five feet to the ground. We rushed over to check for injuries.

Cody said he had just heard two shots from over where the bear was treed. We already knew that our bear had crossed the road and that the other group had then put on the bear, but we weren't sure whether they had seen the bear cross the road or their dogs had struck the track while driving along Patterson Creek Road. Two of my dogs were now high on the other mountain where the bear was treed, and the other one was near my truck.

By now, Cody had successfully rescued the fourth dog. The last dog was still forty feet in the tree when he, too, fell. He hit the ground and rolled down the mountain at least twenty-five yards before stopping. Stunned, we looked at each other, then took off after him. He lay perfectly still on the hillside. We knew he was dead.

At that moment, the dog stood up and started walking toward us. We checked him out and he appeared to be totally okay. We were amazed, but we also knew that dogs, especially hound dogs, could take a beating and keep on going. They were so resilient.

We hiked back down the mountain toward the trucks, which according to the GPS was also where my two dogs were headed. When we got there, all the trucks belonging to the other group were gone except for one, and no one was in it. Someone had placed one of my dogs in my truck. My other two dogs were now only half a mile away, but instead of coming toward me, they were moving rapidly away. I looked at their speed: thirty miles an hour. There was no way they were running that fast. I jumped in my truck and went after them, because I was now sure someone had stolen my dogs and was driving them away. I called Rob and told him this, and he followed me for backup. I was pissed off. I floored the accelerator in pursuit of my dogs.

The GPS showed the dogs—and their thieves—zipping up Caldwell Mountain, so I turned onto Caldwell Mountain Road and headed up to the top, where Price Mountain Road cut to the right. As I topped the mountain, I was driving as fast as I could but still not gaining on them. At the foot of the mountain, they turned left toward Kelly Hollow. It was a road that dead-ended at a forestry gate about five miles down. I'd soon have them trapped.

After three miles, I saw the dogs had stopped. Moments later, a truck with a dog box sped past me in the opposite direction. I was certain it belonged to the dognappers. Rob must have had the same thought, because in my rearview, I saw him whip around and chase after them. I kept driving, and to my great relief, I found my dogs standing in the road, waiting for me.

Later, Rob told me that when he had caught up to them, they denied all of it and said they were just coming out of Kelly

Hollow. But I had continued to the end of the road, and saw no other trucks, so I knew their story was bogus. I filed today's hunt under "You Can't Make This Shit Up."

We went on to kill a few more bears and leave several others in trees, but none of it compared to the excitement earlier in the season, from chasing the bear that should have bled out way before we caught up with it to rescuing five dogs from fifty feet up a partially fallen tree. But perhaps the most exciting moments came when two of our dogs were kidnapped and taken several miles away. Looking back, the thieves probably thought we would figure the dogs had crossed the mountain on their own. But we were tipped off by our tracking equipment, which showed them speeding down the road much faster than they could possibly run. I was just thankful we got them back unharmed.

CHAPTER 11

420

The tales in this chapter are not in chronological order, but they recount some of the most surprising, distressing, or just plain bizarre experiences I've had while bear hunting.

Driving along Kelly Hollow Road with Fox and Gusto one day, we got a hot strike and all our dogs blew up. Fox dropped his tailgate, and his dogs raced away at full cry. They cut to the left and headed toward Patterson Creek. This was in the days of the beep-beep collars, so tracking was limited. Gusto and I also dropped our tailgates, and the dogs sprinted up the mountain. The chase was on.

When they were about halfway up, they cut to the east. We continued along the road, hoping to keep them on the mountain they were on. As they cut east, they were now coming back down the mountain. We continued along the road and heard the dogs coming toward us, barking as loud as they could. Just then, three hundred yards in front of us, the bear crossed the road. It was a good-sized bear, over three hundred pounds. Well, so much for keeping them on the same mountain.

We were almost certain we wouldn't get this bear. First, it had a head start of several hundred yards on the dogs, and second, if it beat them to the top of the mountain, it would then be on private land. The owners didn't allow hunting, other than for a few of their friends, so the only way we would be able to harvest this bear was if the dogs treed it before reaching the top.

We waited on the road until the dogs had crossed over the top of the mountain. The plan was for me to climb the mountain—leaving my pistol in the truck since I would probably be on private land—while Gusto stayed on the Kelly Hollow side and Fox tracked from White Church Road.

When I reached the top, Fox told me the dogs were now treed halfway down the mountain. From my position, I could hear them plainly, but I estimated they were about two miles away. It was a nice day with no wind, and to hear them at full cry from that distance was amazing.

The dogs were well to the east of me, so I started walking in that direction across the top of the mountain. After about a mile, I picked up on a change in the tone of their barking. I was hoping that meant the bear was about to slide out of the tree so the dogs could chase it back onto national forest land again. But five minutes later, two gunshots rang out. Apparently, the change in tone had been because of other hunters arriving at the tree.

I waited on top of the mountain to see where the dogs would go. It seemed like they had split up, with some headed down the mountain toward the hardtop road Fox was on. From what I could tell, two of the dogs were well below me, heading west and moving fast. Normally, they would be barking when keeping that pace, but I didn't hear any barking. Fox thought they might be in a vehicle, moving along a road that wrapped around the mountain and came almost to the top. They seemed to be getting closer, but now they were west of me, so I walked back in the direction I had come from, and my signal got much stronger. Any second now, I would see them.

Just then, two guys stepped out from behind some brush and asked what I was doing.

"Trying to find my dogs," I told them.

"This is private land."

"I know," I said, "but I have the right to track my dogs and retrieve them. They're close by. I'll just get them and head back off the mountain."

To my surprise, the dogs appeared just then, walking toward me. They were followed by another person. I didn't know what was going on, or why, but I was sure that person had been holding the dogs this whole time. I snapped the leads onto the dogs and started off the mountain.

When I was about a quarter of the way down, I noticed they were missing their tracking collars. I told Fox about it. My first thought was that the dogs had pulled their collars off in the brush. But I had been tracking them closely from the top of the mountain, so that probably wasn't the case. Then it hit me: the men on top had stolen the collars. I relayed this to Fox, and he said he was still getting a signal from the collars in that area.

Less than a minute later: *Bang! Bang!*

"Fox," I said on the radio, "I just heard two gunshots."

"And my signal just died on the collars," he replied.

Those men, I knew, had shot the collars to kill the signal. Fox reported the incident to the police, who told him they would be happy to retrieve the collars if we could get a signal on them. But since that wasn't possible, we were told we didn't have a case. Without evidence, it would be their word against ours. We later discovered the bear had been checked in at a check station, so we knew someone with permission to hunt on the land had killed it.

On another occasion, we were hunting at Salt Pond Mountain. We took the dogs in on the ridge that was near the pond, then walked the ridgeline back down toward private land. The ridge was mostly flat, but to get to the private land, we had to cut to the left and down a steep incline.

We didn't get a strike as we were walking along the ridge, but the dogs were beginning to wind toward the next finger ridge on our left, so we started down. The slope was steep and covered in rockslides, and we had made it about halfway down when the dogs went nuts. We cut them loose, and they crossed the finger ridges and headed back toward Salt Pond, full cry. When they were close to the pond, they split up.

The main pack was now treed. Someone on the road chimed in and said he would walk to them because he would be able to reach them faster than we could. We stayed put and waited to hear what was in the tree while we kept track of the other dogs. Soon, we found out the dogs had a fifty-pound cub up the tree.

All the dogs at the tree were on their leads, but there were still four dogs loose, most likely running the sow. According to our tracker, two of the dogs were together and headed toward private land down on Houston Mines Road. The other two appeared to be backtracking toward Salt Pond. We trekked down the ridge to Salt Pond Road, where Rob picked us up. We got word the two dogs that were backtracking were now in their dog box. The signal was increasing in strength as we drove down Houston Mines Road, so we were sure we would have the last two dogs back momentarily.

Soon we arrived at a trailer with a signal so strong we should have been looking right at the dogs. As I hollered for the dogs, there was no change in the signal. After several minutes, I knocked on the door of the trailer and told the person who answered I was looking for my dogs. I asked if I could look around for them, because I thought they might be under the trailer. He gave me permission to look there, but said I couldn't trespass anywhere else on their property. As I looked around under the trailer with my tracking box on, I could tell that not only were the dogs inside the trailer, but on the right end of it. I walked away and reported my findings to Rob and Fox.

We called the police, and while we were waiting for them to show up, one of the occupants of the trailer came out and walked up into the woods. At first, we thought he could be trying to get rid of the tracking collars, but the signal never changed, which added to the mystery.

Thirty minutes later, the dog warden showed up. We explained the situation and told him our dogs were in the trailer, specifically on the right side, or at least they had been thirty minutes ago. Just as he started walking toward the trailer, our two dogs emerged from the left side.

When the warden spoke with the owners, as we

expected, they denied knowing anything about the dogs. After looking under the trailer, he told us he saw a hole in the floor on the left side, which was most likely how they had let the dogs out. But again, with no evidence of them having been in the trailer, there was nothing he could do. This was now the third time our dogs had been kidnapped. We were blessed not to have lost any of our dogs, but Fox did lose two of his tracking collars to bullets.

Another time, I was with Randy, a new friend of Rob's, and we were walking the dogs along the horse trail toward Lee's Gap from Stone Coal Gap Road. We were almost to the middle of Lee's Gap when we got a strike. The dogs exploded, and we turned them loose. They raced up the mountain to the left, and we were sure they would cross over into the gap. But no, they were pulling in the opposite direction. We were overjoyed. Lee's Gap made for a long day of hunting. It was a bear's dream house, but it was extremely rugged, steep, and thick with laurel.

The dogs pulled a quarter of the way up the mountain, then cut back in the direction we had come from. They were now out of hearing range, and since this was before GPS collars, Rob was on the road tracking for us. He said the dogs had cut low on the mountain and might be heading toward private land. Well, we weren't happy to hear that. But since the property belonged to one of Rob's friends, he would try and get permission to go in and get the bear, assuming it was of legal size.

Rob thought the dogs had the bear in a tree because they didn't appear to be moving. Yet mysteriously, none of the treeing switches were going off. He said the dogs sounded good from the road. I could hear the dogs, so I headed straight for them, while Randy stayed a little higher on the mountain. He had his .45 ACP pistol with him and was being careful not to wander onto private property with it.

I continued toward the dogs, and soon I could see a couple of them. No bear yet, which made me think it was bayed up. Moving closer still, a ditch came into view, which was where most of the dogs were. Finally, I saw the bear. This was one huge, pissed-off bear. He was clapping his teeth together and making a chomping sound, which was common when a bear was on the ground and bayed up. It was a shooter all right, about 225 pounds. If Rob could get permission, it would be a nice bear for Randy, who was waiting on the property line for Rob's go-ahead. He was about 150 yards above me, where the tree trunks were painted red, indicating the edge of the national forest.

"Go on in and take care of business, Randy," came Rob's voice on the radio. The owner had given us permission to take the bear. "I'll come around. I think I can get pretty close to you in my truck."

Before Randy could get down to where I was, the bear charged right at him. Fortunately, the bear had about eight dogs on him, so he didn't make it very far—maybe twenty-five feet—before scurrying up a tree. Then he walked out on a limb about twenty feet off the ground. When Randy got to the tree, we stood there for a few minutes enjoying the sight. The bear was still chomping, which was something Randy had never heard. For me, it was unusual to hear it from a bear in a tree. It meant he was getting anxious, and we could see he was ready to come down out of the tree. I told Randy to go ahead and take the bear.

Randy shot twice in the chest cavity, and the bear slid down the tree. He shot again as it came down but missed. The chase was on again—for about twenty feet before the bear treed again. Rob said he had heard the shots and asked if the bear was dead. We told him he had come out of the tree but was treed again. Wait for me before you shoot again, he said. A minute later, Rob showed up and handed Randy his .45-70 rifle. Randy took the finishing shot. It was perfect.

We loaded up all the dogs, then dragged the bear fifty yards to Rob's truck. It had been an exciting day. Baying a bear was by far a bigger adrenaline rush than treeing a bear. It had also been an easy day. We had started by walking the horse trail, which had only the slightest incline and decline. Then we had walked maybe two miles before we got the strike and set the dogs loose. Then another mile before cutting down to the bear. I got to see the dogs baying the bear, which was amazing, then got to see the dogs put the bear up a tree not just once, but two times, from right under the tree. As a bonus, it was a very short drag, after which I caught a ride back to my truck. I couldn't have asked for a better or easier hunt.

One day, we were hunting toward Frank's, and Malcolm Horne was hunting the opposite side of the road from us. We were hunting toward Little Cuba, and Malcolm was hunting toward the county dump. We also had a new guy with us. He was an older guy and a good deer hunter, but he wanted to kill a bear. Since he was a butcher, we called him Butcher Man. We had seen pictures of some of the deer he had killed, and they were quite impressive. Today he was hunting with a lever-action .30-30 rifle.

We hadn't had any luck getting a bear started yet. Malcolm, meanwhile, had already treed a bear and had three of his hunters under the tree. He knew Butcher Man was with us and wanted to kill a bear, so he told us where his dogs were treed: in the holler, just above the first switchback on the trail going up to the top of the mountain.

Rob, Butcher Man, and I headed up to the tree. It was an easy tree to get to, just an uphill climb along the trail then only a hundred yards off the trail at the first switchback. But boy, Butcher Man was breathing hard. He said he normally hunted fields and flat land, so this was a hard pull for him.

The bear was in a scrub pine about twenty feet off the ground, but Butcher Man was having a hard time spotting him. We had him look at it from different angles, and he was finally able to see the bear. He had never seen a bear before and was so excited. He immediately got his gun out, ready to shoot. We told him to sit there for a few minutes, enjoy the bear, and rest a bit so he could get off a good shot. We had plenty of dogs under the bear, so it wouldn't be going anywhere.

After a few minutes, Butcher Man seemed rested but still a little anxious. We found him the best location to shoot from, and he got set up. He took his shot, but it was no good. Knowing he was an experienced deer hunter, we hadn't bothered to back him up. The bear sailed out of the tree, and all the dogs were cut loose again. This bear had a lot of life in him. He bounded down the hill at full speed with the dogs on his heels. We all rushed down the mountain after him, with me in the lead.

Just then, I heard a gunshot behind me. My first thought was someone had seen the bear and took a shot. My next thought was there was no way someone had seen the bear, because the dogs were still well below us. I could hear them at full cry, probably about to cross Stone Coal Gap Road. I looked behind me in the direction of the gunshot. There was some commotion among the guys.

"Dale, I thought you were dead!" Rob called out to me.

I gave him a quizzical look, and he came down and explained what had happened. They had been running, and he noticed Butcher Man's gun was still cocked, so he told him to lower the hammer. Butcher Man attempted to do this, but with the gun pointed straight in my direction. Sure enough, his thumb slipped and the gun went off. Rob was just waiting for me to fall. We were happy everyone was okay.

Just before we got to the road, three more gunshots rang out. One of Malcolm's men, who was down in the creek with the dogs and the bear, had fired at the bear point blank. The bear was dead. But not before it had mauled one of the dogs, who was lying on the ground, bleeding from a chest wound. They rushed it to the veterinarian, and later that evening, we learned it wasn't the bear that had injured the dog. One of the bullets had gone through the bear and hit the dog. The vet was mad because she thought someone had intentionally shot it. She admonished the hunters for not being careful enough, and told them anytime they were in close range with a bear and dogs, they needed to be much more cautious.

We sat down and had a long talk with Butcher Man. We let him know the reason we didn't back him up at the tree was because we thought he was a great shot after hearing about all the deer he had killed. He admitted his eyesight wasn't what it used to be, and seeing through the open sights had been a challenge because he normally used a rifle with a scope. We asked why he had been so anxious, and he said he was never that way around deer, but seeing the bear had made him nervous.

Rob told him what concerned us most was running down the mountain without making sure his gun was safe, nearly killing me in the process. He was very rattled over this. He explained that he had still been nervous at the time, which was why his thumb had slipped off the hammer. We could tell he was very upset knowing he had almost killed me. But we didn't stop there. Had he made a clean kill, we told him, the bear wouldn't have run down the mountain, and there would have been no injured dog.

Butcher Man was a very nice guy, but that day he realized bear hunting wasn't his cup of tea and decided he wouldn't be hunting with us anymore. To his credit, he helped Malcolm out with his two thousand–dollar vet bill.

Although I wasn't there for it, this next story was a memorable one for our club, the North Mountain Hunt Club. It started as a normal day, first going up to Frank's and then hunting the mountain to the right toward Craig County. J.C. Laprade, Cody Hosey, Kevin Heavner, Striker, and a few other hunters were taking the dogs up the trail: Benny, Dozer, Cooper, Jessie Jr. ("J.J."), and several others.

They topped out and cut west toward Little Cuba. As they moved across the top of the mountain, Benny started wandering to the left, back down toward the road. He opened up a little, so they cut him and Dozer loose, even though it didn't appear to be a hot track, and the two dogs went down the hill together.

After thirty minutes, Dozer came back on his own. They put him back on his lead, and Cody told J.C. he would go down and get Benny. He caught Benny several hundred yards off the road. Cody got Rob to take him and Benny down the road a ways. He told J.C. to keep heading in the same direction, and he would cut back up the mountain to get in front of him and the dogs.

After he dropped off Cody and Benny, Rob reported seeing a large bear come off the mountain and just stand in the middle of the road for an extended period of time. He told everyone to come off the mountain but not to let any of the dogs loose until they got to where he was on the road.

As the group headed down the mountain toward Rob, J.C. slipped and fell. He gave his dogs to one of the other hunters and told him to go on ahead and he would be down as soon as he could. But as J.C. came limping off the mountain, he said he thought he had a broken leg. He assured everyone he would be okay and told the others to go and get the job done.

White Bear stood by at the bottom, waiting for his son to come out of the woods. Rob was with everyone else down on the road, and he told them where the bear had last been. The dogs were released, and they ran down to the creek, where they encountered the bear, who then came running up from the creek and crossed the road. The dogs walked him up the opposite mountain in the direction of the dump.

Cody predicted they would tree the bear with that many dogs walking it. Rob disagreed, thinking the bear would just continue to walk and fight the dogs. Rob took Cody, Striker, and a few others up to Frank's and told them to continue to the top of the mountain so they could be there when the bear crossed. But by the time they reached the top, the bear had already crossed and was heading toward the dump.

Striker hung back at Frank's while Rob sped around to the dump. There, he picked up a beep-beep signal on the dogs. He knew they were down low but couldn't tell exactly where, so he drove to the power line parking lot.

By now, Striker had come around the mountain. He told Rob he had a good signal on the dogs and could hear them above the furnace. By the time Rob got to the furnace, he had a good signal on the dogs, too, but wasn't able to hear them.

Striker urged him to get in there and take the bear,

but Rob said all his guns were still on the mountain. Striker handed Rob his .270 rifle, and Rob continued along the logging road. After three hundred yards, Rob said he could hear them coming toward him. Knowing they would be crossing the trail in front of him, he dropped to one knee and assumed his shooting position.

Rob squeezed off a shot as soon as the bear stepped into the trail. The bear turned and looked back at the dogs, as if blaming them for the pain he had just felt. When the bear turned around again, Rob shot two more times. When he went to bolt in another bullet, he realized he was out of ammo.

"Hey, Striker," Rob called over the radio, "I'm out of bullets, and I—"

BOOM!

Rob whipped around to see where this loud sound had come from. There was Kevin Heavner, his .44 Magnum pistol still smoking. Kevin shot again, and it looked like a hit. But the bear was still on his feet, so Kevin shot one more time, and the bear went down.

Rob took the gun from Kevin, ran down to the bear, and put one more in his head. He didn't think the last shot was needed but wanted to make sure the bear was dead.

Rob's next concern was checking on his dogs. Benny and Dozer appeared to be okay, but Cooper had a large bite mark over his spinal column, in the middle of his back. The rest of the dogs also seemed all right, but J.J. was missing. Rob picked up the radio and asked Cody, who was still on the mountain, to search for J.J. Cody said he had a strong signal on her.

Striker caught up with Rob and pointed to the tree right next to him, wondering who had shot it. Rob realized that Kevin's first shot had hit the tree right at head level. He had been lucky. From that day on, Kevin wasn't allowed to carry a pistol while hunting with us.

By now, Cody had found J.J., who had an open chest wound and fractured ribs. He carried her back to White Bear's truck. Kevin and Striker rounded up the rest of the dogs and took them back to Striker's truck. J.C. was in pain, but he insisted on accompanying the group to the vet. He and his dad dropped Cody off to go with Striker and Kevin up the mountain to help with the bear.

Rob, meanwhile, took Cooper to the vet, then stopped by his house to get a drag sled for the bear, because he knew the guys wouldn't be able to get the bear off the mountain without it. When he got back to the furnace, he found the five of them just sitting there, not even trying to move the bear. They had tied their dog leads around the bear but still couldn't budge it.

Once they managed to position the bear on the sled, three of them pulled it while one kept them moving straight with a dog lead on the bear's hind foot. Back at Rob's truck, it took everyone's strength to hoist the bear up onto the truck. Rob took it to the check station to get it weighed. You may have heard of the movie *Cocaine Bear*. Well, we named this bear Marijuana Bear when we saw its field-dressed weight: 420 pounds.

Later, everyone met up at Rob's house to take the bear to our hunt club to skin it. J.C. was there, still in pain, but insisting he wasn't leaving until the bear was in the cooler. Afterward, White Bear took him to the ER, where it was confirmed his right leg was broken, and a cast was put in place. Cooper underwent back surgery, which fortunately healed up well. J.J. had three broken ribs, one of which was pressing against her heart. She had to have several surgeries, and we never hunted her again. Dozer, sadly, had grown quite old, and this was to be his last hunt before he died.

I wish I could have been a part of this hunt. It's not every day you get to kill Marijuana Bear. For Rob, it was an extremely costly hunt: the vet bill was over four thousand dollars, plus a life-size taxidermy bill of another four grand.

Cooper continued hunting for years, but after every long run, the top of his back would start to bleed. It didn't seem to cause him any issues, but several years after the initial injury, a piece of his backbone worked its way out from under the skin. It was about a quarter inch in diameter and three quarters of an inch long. This was what had been causing the bleeding every time he ran a long distance. We kept that piece of bone on display in the clubhouse, near the life-size bear mount.

CHAPTER 12
Row, Row, Row Your Boat

Chase season came around again, and we were heading up to Frank's. We planned to send the dogs up the left side of the road once we got there. Rob opened his tailgate to let the dogs out, and up the trail they went. Then, everyone else dropped their tailgates, and all the dogs were now racing up the trail.

Once the dogs had topped out, they continued across the top of the mountain but soon split up into three different groups. They were all trying to find a track, but we weren't hearing any of the dogs opening up, and no bark meters had gone off.

Maybell and Reno were now two high peaks past where they had first topped out, and their bark meters were showing sixty barks a minute. They cut off to the south side of the mountain and headed toward the furnace.

Now at sixty to eighty barks a minute, but hardly moving, we thought they had hit a big boy and started walking him. All the other dogs were now on the north side of the mountain, where they had hit a track and started running a cub. Rob caught them all when they ran past him on the road.

I went around to the furnace. Maybell and Reno were now high on the mountain and moving toward the power line. Rob's son Tyler headed up the trail at the power line to try to get on top. At the speed the dogs were going, it would be a while before they reached Tyler. When Tyler topped out, he could hear them off to his right. He walked in that direction but had no dogs to join with Maybell and Reno.

The bear, meanwhile, seemed to be following the contour line at 2,800 feet of elevation. We told Tyler to drop down to that elevation before the dogs got to him. As he moved down the mountain, he heard the dogs coming toward him. But before the bear got to him, it climbed to the top and crossed to the opposite side of the mountain. He caught a glimpse of it and told us it was over four hundred pounds.

Rob and I went around past Frank's and were able to locate the dogs. We were surprised that even on the north side, the bear was still following the 2,800-foot contour line. Whether this was by coincidence or not, we weren't sure. The dogs continued to follow the same contour line, but since it was so hot out, they were not barking as much now. Soon, they stopped barking altogether and didn't appear to be moving. After climbing to the top of the mountain, they were too hot and tired to continue.

It wasn't a bad opening day. We had seen two bears, one of which was over four hundred pounds, and Rob had to pull a pack of dogs off a cub. The bear Tyler had seen was a nice one, and I hoped it would still be around come kill season.

That season, we ran him at least two more times. We named him 2,800-Foot Bear due to the fact that he liked to stay at the 2,800-foot contour line. It was even more strange because it didn't matter which side of the mountain he was on. We tried to get in place to see the bear, but we could never get a lot of hound pressure on him. We usually had two or three dogs on him at the most. He was a smart bear, but then again, there weren't any large, dumb bears out there. During the season, we ran several other bears and treed some smaller bears, as well as a few sows with cubs.

Kill season was now open. Hoping 2,800-Foot Bear was still in the area, we sent the dogs back up the trail near Frank's that went toward the dump. They reached the top of the mountain and continued across until they got to the second knob. There, the dogs opened up and the bark meters went off at eighty barks a minute. They had hit a hot track, and now we had Reno, Maybell, Puppy, and Forrest on the bear. They dropped off the south side and headed east toward the furnace.

Rob stayed at Frank's in case they came back across the top of the mountain, while Cody Morris headed to the furnace. Meanwhile, I made my way to the dump. I shut off the truck to listen, and I could hear them putting off a lot of mouth from high on the mountain. I couldn't help but notice they were on the 2,800-foot contour line. Had we found the big boy? And during kill season to boot?

The dogs had slowed down considerably and were now creeping toward the furnace. They pressed on for nearly forty-five minutes, then cut down the mountain a short distance. Then they changed direction and headed west to climb back up to the 2,800-foot contour line. This bear was smart, and he knew that if he continued in this direction, he would be forced to cross a road at some point, which meant more dogs would be packed on to him.

I realized I would probably be in the driver's seat on this bear as I rushed up the road to the power line parking lot. If I could climb up the mountain and get in position on the 2,800-foot contour line, I may be able to get a shot on the big boy. It had been a good acorn crop, so I was willing to bet he was pushing five hundred pounds now. Initially I couldn't hear the dogs, but once I was higher on the mountain, I could hear them coming.

I wasn't sure if I could get high enough on the trail by the time they crossed it. In the old days, I would have been up there already, but I was now sixty years old and had been diagnosed with alpha-gal syndrome the year before.

Alpha-gal is a tick-borne disease where sufferers cannot eat any mammalian meat. The disease sucks. People can go into anaphylactic shock and even die from eating steak, or in the most severe cases, just by being around meat as it's cooking.

My main symptoms were acute, multi-joint pain, extreme tiredness, and gastrointestinal issues like nausea, vomiting, and diarrhea. After staying away from mammalian meat, my symptoms improved but didn't disappear. I still had some joint pain. I got very tired upon exertion and stayed tired. I felt blessed that I was much improved, but the disease had definitely impacted how fast I could move.

The dogs hadn't crossed the trail yet, but they were getting close. I was three hundred yards away, pushing as hard as I could, but I couldn't get up there before they crossed the trail. I continued to the top of the mountain, then headed west across the top. The dogs were 0.8 miles in front of me. I felt like I could close the distance since they were walking the bear, and it was much easier walking along the top of the mountain than climbing up. But I couldn't close the gap, and they remained the same distance in front of me.

I headed toward Turkey Trail while the dogs climbed up the south side of the mountain and crossed over the top. Soon, they were at the 2,800-foot contour line on the north side. By now, I had managed to get closer to them, and I was only 0.6 miles away from 2,800-Foot Bear. Gaining on them had put a little extra pep in my step.

But once the bear hit the north side of the mountain, his pace picked up. I was now a whole mile from the bear, and it didn't look like I would be able to catch up with him. Rob had Tyler and Cody go up Grouse Trail, which was just past Turkey Trail, to try and get in front of the bear. I was discouraged and tired, and it was getting late. When I finally made it to Turkey Trail, Rob asked me to come down from the mountain. I had mixed emotions about doing that, because if they killed the bear, I would have to climb back to the top again to help drag it off the mountain.

By the time I was halfway down the mountain, it was getting dark, and I had to put my headlamp on. It was completely dark by the time I made it to the wildlife road. I let Rob know I was out on the road, and he said he would come pick me up after he got Cody and Tyler out of the woods.

When they showed up, Tyler told me what had happened. He was out in front of Cody and knew the bear liked the 2,800-foot contour line, so he dropped down to that elevation. He said he could hear the bear coming through the laurel about a hundred yards away, breaking brush and making a lot of noise. Then the bear took off in what sounded like a sprint to the top of the mountain and crossed over to the south side. He felt certain the bear had scented him, which was why it had bolted to the top of the mountain. He was able to put a couple of the dogs on leads while two of the dogs stayed on the bear. When it got dark, Cody and Tyler called the last two dogs off the bear, then headed down Grouse Trail to the trucks.

We ran 2,800-Foot Bear at least three more times during the season. On one occasion, Tyler saw the bear treed from a distance, but before he could get there, the bear came out of the tree. Tyler only had a 10mm pistol, which he unloaded on him, but the bear didn't appear to have been hit. And we knew he hadn't been fatally wounded because we ran him again on another day.

This was the only bear I'd ever seen that only liked running at a certain elevation on the mountain. I started to believe he was secretly using GPS to know his elevation.

At Frank's again one day, we hit the mountain on the right with the plan to hunt toward Lee's Gap. Once on top, we cut to the right and had gone maybe a mile before we hit a hot track. We cut all the dogs loose, and they left out at full cry, speeding off the mountain toward Craig Creek.

We decided to head back to the trucks and drive around. When we got to the end of Hebron Road, we picked up a beep-beep signal on the dogs. They were down near the creek and seemed to be stopped, but none of the treeing switches were going off.

I headed in their direction with my .44 Magnum pistol. At first, I could hear them, but once they dropped off the mountain, I had to rely on my tracking box. By now, Barry was coming in behind me.

I continued to the top of the next finger ridge, where I could now hear them. There were two dogs down there about half a mile away from me. They were at full cry, but the treeing switches still weren't going off.

Two finger ridges later, I was right above them. They

were down in a deep V holler, and I decided to go down the left finger ridge and drop down to the V from there to get below them. I still hadn't seen the dogs or the bear, but for two hounds, they were sure putting off some mouth. I got down almost to the center of the V and spotted them about forty feet above me.

I knew I was getting close to the national forest line, but I was happy to see red paint below me, telling me I was still on public land. The bear was in the V holler, backed up against debris and a blown-down tree about ten feet tall. I was looking at a boar bear that probably weighed 350 pounds. The bear had only one escape route, which was coming down through the V holler past me and the dogs. I called Rob on the radio and described the scene.

"How many dogs are there?" he asked. "Are they ours?"

"There are two dogs here, Rob, but I only recognize one of them."

"There's another group hunting the area with dogs, so the other one is probably theirs. And what about our other dog?"

I checked on the other dog I'd been tracking. "He's in the area," I replied, "but I can't see him."

"Okay, the other group is trying to get down there, too, so stay back and hopefully the dogs will keep the bear at bay. But protect those dogs. I don't need to tell you what to do if the bear comes at them. I know you'll take care of business."

The bear was chomping and clicking his teeth. I loved seeing a bayed bear, and I sat there for a while watching the dogs do their work. But I also knew this was the most dangerous situation the dogs could be in. The bear was looking for an escape route, and with me being there, he would surely try to get away. I had my pistol cocked and ready should I need it.

"Dale, this is Barry. I'm getting close to you."

I probably should have turned my radio off, because in that instant, the bear charged the dogs. Then he came running down the V holler and straight toward me. When he was twenty-five feet from me, I had a clear shot at the bear's chest. I pulled the trigger. He stopped and just stood there. I shot again. He went down, and the dogs sailed in on him. As I walked up, I could see he was still breathing, so I placed one more shot in his neck, at the base of his skull.

"That's a nice boar," Barry said when he showed up. We rolled it over together. It was actually a sow bear—the largest I had ever seen. I told Rob we had better get a lot more people for the drag out. Hold tight, he said. He would let us know something shortly.

He called us back to tell us Cody Hosey had a canoe, so we could drag the bear downhill to Craig Creek and then float it out. Barry and I tied all the dogs up. There were a total of four dogs: two of ours and two that belonged to the other hunting group.

Given the size of the bear, we weren't sure if we could drag it at all. But since it was downhill, it wasn't too bad of a drag. We cut to our left along the creek and came out on a road about half a mile away. We then hiked back up and brought the dogs closer to the creek to wait for Cody. He had to go home to get his canoe, so we knew it would take a while.

As it turned out, we heard Cody approaching well before we saw him. He was singing, "Row, row, row your boat, gently down the stream" as he paddled. Barry and I cracked up.

Cody pulled the canoe up to the bank and all three of us worked to load the bear into it. Cody then paddled down to a ford on the creek, where Rob met him and loaded the bear into his truck. Barry and I led all four dogs along the creek until we could get to the road to be picked up. I must say this was the first time our group had floated a bear out.

The sow weighed 300 pounds on the nose and was eighteen years old, the Department of Game and Inland Fisheries determined from the tooth I had pulled and sent to them.

We had several more good hunts during kill season that year. We killed three bears, including one that was 150 pounds and another close to 200 pounds. We really were trying to get

2,800-Foot Bear, but it wasn't meant to be this year. Maybe next year.

Overall, I enjoyed this year's hunts. By far the most exciting part was the adrenaline rush of being that close to a bayed bear. I lived off that feeling. And of course, the funniest part was Cody paddling down the creek singing, "Row, Row, Row Your Boat," giving Barry and me a hearty laugh.

CHAPTER 13
Rob as a Maine Houndsman

About fifteen years ago, Rob and a couple of the other guys from our club decided to go hunting up in Maine, and they took Rob's dogs with them. Everyone who went came back with a bear the first year, and they talked about hunting in Maine as though it were totally different than hunting in Virginia.

Oxbow Outfitters, a company that offered guided hunts, asked Rob to come back to Maine and be a houndsman for them. This was a person with experience handling hounds and during a hunt would keep track of the dogs at all times to make sure they were going after the right animal.

Rob said he would think about it, and a couple of years later, he did it. As a houndsman, Rob had to have an in-state guide with him while using his dogs to hunt for his customers, but eventually he became certified as a guide himself.

As a Maine Guide, Rob had to know which bear hunting methods were allowed in the state. The first method of hunting was over bait site, where thirty-gallon barrels filled with food were set out to attract bears. The bait consisted of corn, donuts, and bread, sometimes sweetened with a little honey or other attractors. Every evening, someone would go around to each site and set out fresh bait.

Each site was equipped with ground blinds and tree stands, as well as cameras, so hunters could see the bears in advance. Hunters would then choose the bait sites they wanted to hunt, and Rob's company would drive them there. The weapons a hunter was permitted to use included bows and arrows, crossbows, rifles, pistols, and muzzleloaders, depending on the season.

The second method Maine allowed was hunting with dogs, and Rob used his own dogs to help his clients find bears. Often, this involved getting a bear started at a bait site that currently had no one hunting over it. A tablet in his truck allowed him to see each bait site and the bears that had been visiting. Using this information, his clients would select the bear they wanted to run.

Rob told stories of a massive bear, well over six hundred pounds, that had killed many dogs. He refused to use his dogs to go after that bear. One hunter, excited about the prospect of a six hundred–pound bear, asked Rob if he could use his own dogs since Rob wouldn't use his. "That's your call," Rob told him. "But if you like your dogs, I wouldn't do it." The hunter really wanted to run that bear, so they pulled up to the bait site. Well, once the client saw that bruiser, he changed his mind. Another hunter also wanted to run that bear and agreed to use his own dogs. Unfortunately, it didn't turn out well.

The third and most controversial way of hunting, which I didn't even realize you could do, was trapping bears in a snare. When a bear set foot in the snare, the device would grab the bear's leg so it couldn't run away. The "hunter" would then come in and shoot the bear that, again, had no way to escape. Guides needed to have a special license and extensive knowledge about which types of snares were legal and which were not. Personally, I didn't like this method of bear hunting. In fact, I didn't even consider it hunting. Rob felt the same way, and as a Maine Guide, he hunted exclusively with dogs.

In Virginia, there was no limit on the number of dogs you could use while hunting bear. In Maine, there was a six-dog limit, upped from four a few years before. But according to Rob, bear hunting in Maine was quite different, and fewer dogs were required to get the job done. He normally used two or three dogs, and a fourth only on occasion. In the part of Maine where Rob hunted, it was a fifty-fifty split between killing bears while they were up in trees and as they crossed roads. And in Maine, it was legal to shoot from the road, unlike in Virginia.

In Maine, Rob explained, the roads ran east-west and north-south in a grid, with about three miles between roads, which formed squares they called blocks. The terrain was not mountainous like in Virginia, but instead consisted of rolling hills and bogs. Many of these bogs looked only ankle deep, Rob told me, until you stepped into one and found yourself up to your hips in the muck.

On one hunt, a bear was killed right in the middle of one of the blocks. When the other hunters tried to get to the bear, they discovered the underbrush was so thick they couldn't walk through it, and they had to cut a path all the way to the tree with machetes.

Usually, they would be able to summon other hunters from their camp, who would come and help them drag the bear out. However, Rob had no means of communication from where he was. So the three of them did their best to drag the bear out, but the rugged terrain made it a huge challenge.

They kept expecting help to show up, but no one arrived until almost dark, and they still had a ways to go. The bear weighed 250 pounds, which made for a long drag out, but in the end, the client was able to take the bear home. Rob said that was probably his longest day in Maine.

On another hunt, Rob was hiking up to where his dogs had treed a bear and found he could go no further: the tree was on top of a towering rock bluff. Meanwhile, the guide was coming up from the opposite side and ran into another rock bluff, making passage impossible. They both looked for a way to get to the dogs, but before they could, the bear came out of the tree and the chase was back on. They weren't able to stop the bear again that day.

Whenever he could, Rob liked to make hunting as easy as possible. If he was near a road with a client who was a good shot, he liked to get the hunter set up, then wait for the bear to step out into the road. If the hunter made a clean kill, there was no need to drag the bear at all. About half of his clients were able to get their bears this way.

Rob encountered plenty of other animals, too, such

as coyotes and bobcats. He had to be very careful about the animals his dogs chased, though, both for their safety and to avoid fines. Fortunately, his dogs had never come in contact with any porcupines, but he had seen a couple during his time in Maine.

Also, the game commission in Maine was very strict about enforcing rules, and if a dog was caught chasing a moose or a lynx, Rob could be fined up to ten thousand dollars.

While Rob was in Maine, the biggest bear he had heard of being killed was a whopping 508 pounds. The smallest was just 22 pounds, and Rob was quick to add that it had happened at a bait site, and he wasn't there. I had a hard time understanding why anyone would take a 22-pound bear. Even raccoons got bigger than that. But because Maine had no size limit on bears, hunters could shoot any bear they wanted to. Maine also had no regulations on shooting a sow with cubs. You could take any of them. You could take all of them if you had several hunters.

In my opinion, regulations should be in place for these scenarios. I am more comfortable with the 100-pound limit that Virginia has. I truly don't think I will pull a trigger again on a bear under 400 pounds. I'll help anyone that wants a bear to get one, but the work starts when you pull the trigger.

When Oxbow Outfitters folded, Rob got on with Big Machias Lake Camps. What follows are three of Rob's most memorable hunts with them.

One year, Cody Hosey went to Maine to be a houndsman for Rob and help him with baiting. Cody had brought several of his dogs along hoping to hunt them, but that week, it so happened that all of Rob's clients had tagged out by Wednesday, meaning they had used all the hunting tags they'd been allotted. Since Cody never got a chance to cut his dogs loose on a bear, he and Rob decided to have a just-for-fun hunt to let Cody run his dogs.

The next day, they pulled up to a bait site on Reality Road. Rob looked at his tablet and saw that a nice-sized bear had visited the site just a couple of hours prior. Rob told

Cody to take three of his dogs down to the site to get the track started. Cody took his dogs down and walked all around the bait site, but his dogs couldn't seem to find a track. So he went back up to the truck and told Rob to let *his* dogs get the bear started. Rob let Reno and DJ out, and immediately they took out on the track. They found the bear lying not two hundred yards from the bait site.

The dogs were now looping back up to Reality Road, so Rob and Cody hustled to get up to where the bear and dogs were going to cross. Moments later, the bear crossed sixty yards in front of them, but the dogs hadn't crossed yet.

Rob stopped his truck right where the bear had crossed and told Cody to put three of his dogs on the bear. Cody dumped the box with his dogs, but with Rob's two dogs, they were now over the limit of dogs on the ground. So, Rob caught Reno and DJ, while Cody's dogs went on to tree the bear only four hundred yards off the road. That's when they both realized neither had a gun with them. They walked to the tree anyway and admired the nice-sized bear they had caught. Cody looked over at Rob. "Now that's how you tree a bear," he said.

Another year, our mutual friend Johnny Lanier was up in Maine. Johnny was often out west taking clients on hunts for various species of big game, but this week he was with Rob, helping out as his houndsman. Rob was checking the bait at a crossover bait site and noticed that a very large bear had visited the site at 1:15 a.m. Johnny was checking another bait site and saw that the same bear had visited at 4:15 a.m, so Rob told him to put his dogs on the bear from that site, since it was much fresher. Given the size of the bear, he warned Johnny to use only two dogs. The more dogs there were, the more emboldened they would feel to get close to the bear. Two dogs would be more likely to stay at a safe distance.

Johnny took his dogs, Buck and Bear Mutt, down to the bait site, and they hit the track. As the dogs cold trailed the bear, they crossed a gravel road and headed into a swamp. Once in the swamp, they jumped the bear, then walked it to the intersection of two gravel roads, where Johnny, the clients, and a fellow houndsman, Jeff, were waiting for the bear to cross the road. The brush on the edge of the swamp crackled and bristled, and the bear appeared, just before turning around and walking right back into the swamp.

But a short time later, Rob spotted the bear running in the brush parallel to a grass road, so he sped around to get in front of the bear. Once in front of the bear, he coaxed all the dogs in his dog box to start barking to make the bear think there were more dogs coming for it. And he could tell from his GPS that it was working: Buck and Bear Mutt were now headed back down to South Branch Road.

The clients were now in Jeff's truck, and Rob backed quickly down the grass road while hollering at Johnny: "It's about to cross the road close to South Branch!"

The others were set up and ready as Rob sped in their direction. But as he drove, he lost track of how close he was to South Branch Road before realizing with sudden terror that he would be in the line of fire in mere seconds. He slammed on his brakes. As Rob screeched to a stop, multiple shots rang out, followed by a short pause, then more shots, then another pause, then one final shot.

"All clear!" someone shouted. "Bear dead!" They had dropped the bear in the middle of the road—and it was a big one, weighing in at 486 pounds.

One day, Rob and another Maine Guide, Eric, went on a hunt for fun after all their clients had tagged out for the week. When they checked the cameras, Rob saw a bear he wanted to run and put three of his dogs out at the bait site. The dogs trailed for a while, then jumped the bear and ran it toward Trappers Run on 25-Mile Cutoff Road.

Rob and Eric rushed to where they knew the bear would cross the road, but they missed him. They sped down to 30-Mile Road, where they saw brush moving in a thicket. Rob figured the bear had smelled them and turned around again. He put three more dogs on the bear, bringing him up to the limit of six dogs. The bear then made a loop and tried to cross the road in front of him. They hopped back into the truck, but it wouldn't start, so Rob handed Eric his .45-70 rifle and Eric ran to the top of the hill. Rob had to stifle a giggle seeing Eric run because he reminded him of Chumlee from the reality series *Pawn Stars*.

When Eric reached the top of the hill, the bear was already crossing the road. Eric raised his gun, aimed, and ... *click*. He had forgotten to take the second safety off. But he took it off and still managed to shoot the bear. One of the dogs, Donkey, ran into the road and started chewing on the bear, then ran off to follow the back track of the bear.

With the bear dead, they turned their attention to getting the truck started. All Rob heard was a clicking sound when he turned the key, so he rummaged around in his truck and found an old leaf spring he had broken a week before while driving on these rough Maine roads. He used it to tap on the starter while Eric turned the key. The engine roared to life.

In order to load the bear onto the truck, Rob would first have to remove the bait buckets stored on the top. He drove back down the road to the bait site where they had started the bear earlier. Rob pulled in and parked the truck, remembering Eric's warning not to turn the engine off. He unloaded all the bait buckets, then headed back to Eric and the bear.

Loading a bear this size onto the truck was going to be a tough job for the two of them, but Rob was certain that any time now, a moose hunter would be coming along this road and they would have some help. There were moose hunters driving down this road all day long, Rob insisted, but after some time, none had come along. It was time to improvise again.

Rob found two ratchet straps in his truck, and working in unison, the two of them were able to lift the bear up onto the tailgate. Good enough, Rob thought. That was about as far as they would be able to move the bear with their makeshift system. Back at the camp, they hung the bear and gutted it. Then, they unloaded all the dogs except Donkey, who was probably back at the bait site. Sure enough, Donkey was waiting for them there, so they put him back in the dog box and loaded the bait buckets back onto the top of the truck. Rob said this was his most memorable hunt in Maine and the story he told most often when someone asked what hunting was like up there.

◊

I asked Rob if he had any closing comments for the chapter that I was dedicating to him and his Maine adventures. As a matter of fact, yes, he said. He would love to see more people rally in support of hound hunters. There is already plenty of proposed legislation that would affect hound hunters across our country, and without more popular support, the timeless tradition of hunting with dogs could be severely restricted in some areas, and even outlawed entirely in certain states.

In Virginia, for example, the game commission is arguing that hounds are the reason for mange in bears, which is most certainly not the case. In fact, it's the opposite: many houndsmen have said they have more fear of their dogs catching mange from a bear. Bear hounds are expensive, and their owners take incredibly good care of them. If a hound were to get mange, it would be treated immediately and there would be no danger of it spreading to bears. Nonetheless, Virginia is using this argument to impose new rules on hound hunters.

Another complaint comes from landowners, who feel as though our dogs have no right to trespass on their land. In Virginia, we have a lot of new people moving in who are not familiar with hound hunting. They know nothing about our traditions and don't care to.

The solution to this problem could lie in technology, which gives us the ability to train our dogs to stay off private property through the use of collars that will lightly shock a dog if it goes beyond a certain point. Our GPS devices even allow us to mark off a specific area, much like an invisible fence.

It works like this: When a dog is approaching one of the boundaries, the collar will first beep to warn the dog to turn around. If the dog does not respond, the collar will administer a shock, starting with the lowest amount of electrical stimulation, and if necessary, increasing to the maximum. In this way, we learn the level of shock each of our dogs responds to, knowing that some dogs need a little more juice than others. But over time, the dogs will get shocked less often as they come to associate the beeping with the need to change direction.

We could set up these invisible fences in areas where we know landowners have issues with dogs being on their land. However, this will only work when the collar is in communication with the handheld GPS unit, so it won't work a hundred percent of the time. All the same, it could prevent the majority of incidents.

I encourage anyone reading this book to reach out to your local delegate or senator to voice your support of hound hunters across the country. Many states are voting on bills that could outlaw hunting with dogs or, at the very least, make it difficult to continue our tradition. While the latest one in Virginia didn't pass, more proposals are undoubtedly on the way, and I would like to ask each of you to reach out in support of our tradition, which goes back to even before the time of Daniel Boone, who also hunted with hounds.

CHAPTER 14

Killer Bear

This year, our hunting group had a good chase season, mostly running sows with cubs or just small bears. We didn't see many big bears, but we still put a good number of bears up the bush.

In his second year of bear hunting, my grandson Landon was making his way through the woods a little better now. Landon saw his first bear in a tree last year, which was his first time hunting with us. He had moved up the list and was now third in line to kill a bear. It was a system that assigned club members a rank based on time hunting with us while giving priority to those who had never killed a bear.

First day of kill season, we had dogs going in from different directions, and it wasn't long before we had two chases going. Landon and I were on the road, tracking Rob's dogs as they treed a bear on top of the mountain. The guys who had led the dogs in said they would backtrack and see what they had up the bush.

Corey Firestone, who had his own bear hunting group but hunted with us sometimes, was with us that day. His dogs had treed a bear about two hundred yards off the road, and now he was on his way in with the person who was going to kill the bear. "It's a shooter," Corey said when they got there. The guy with him proceeded to shoot the bear.

The two of them dragged it out to the truck, which didn't take long since it was all downhill. The shooter took the bear to the cabin to skin and hang in the cooler. We estimated its weight at about 175 pounds.

When Tyler and the rest of the group caught up with Rob's dogs on top of the mountain, they saw a shootable bear as they approached the tree. But as they drew closer, they realized it was a sow with two forty-pound cubs. The cubs were higher in the tree than the sow, which was why they didn't see them at first. This was normal; sows usually stayed lower in the tree to protect their cubs. Tyler and the others sat and rested for a few minutes, then headed back across the top of mountain to find another track.

Corey got a strike on a second bear, and since he only had one other person with him, Landon and I went down the road to help track his dogs. It wasn't long until they pulled up treed, so Landon and I started the mile-and-a-half hike in. The bear had treed in the lowlands, so it was mostly flat or downhill, but never more than a gentle climb.

Corey was ahead of us and beat us to the tree by a few minutes. I wasn't sure who was with him, but he didn't shoot the bear. When we arrived at the tree, Corey and I looked the bear over. We believed it to be of legal weight, but barely, so we agreed not to shoot it. It was probably 110 pounds at best.

The following Saturday, Rob brought his good friend Daniel Perdue, who was visiting for the week with his eleven-year-old son, Wyatt. We were hoping Wyatt would get a bear today since they wouldn't be here long.

Both Rob's and Daniel's dogs started up the mountain on their leads, hoping to find a track on some prime, private land that adjoined the national forest, an area we had special permission to hunt. They got a strike right away and cut the dogs loose one by one. The dogs ran the bear straight up the mountain, and when they were close to the top, eight of the dogs showed treed. Rob walked with Wyatt toward the tree. From two hundred yards away, Rob could tell it was a shooter.

They continued walking, but at 150 yards from the tree, the bear jumped down and the chase was on again. It took less than ten minutes to tree it again. The dogs were now halfway down the mountain, below and to the west of where Rob was. He told me he was about nine hundred yards away, but the terrain was steep and overgrown, so it would take him a while to get there. As they approached the bear this time, it jumped out of the tree again and bounded down the mountain, looking like it might cross the road onto private land. Once the bear was down low in the thicket, it sounded like the dogs had caught it and were now fighting it.

They were less than seventy-five yards from the road, and I was driving beside them. But my truck caused them to turn and head east. All the dogs who had been above me as I drove down the road were now showing treed. I was shocked to see the bear only a hundred yards off the road, in a small tree, and not very high up.

I hollered at Rob and told him where the bear was treed, and that I could see it from the road. Fortunately, he told me, it was still on the private land we had come in on, so we had permission to hunt it. Landon asked if he could shoot the bear, but I told him Rob wanted Wyatt to shoot it since they were only here for a short period of time.

We knew a small tree wouldn't hold the bear for very long, so Rob asked me to go to the trucks and get his and Daniel's remaining eight dogs to pack to the others. I did that, and I added my three dogs to the mix, too, then made it back down to where the bear was treed. When the dogs got close to the bear, it made one last-ditch effort to escape. It came down from the tree and headed straight west, back into the thicket. But with fifteen dogs chasing it and chewing on its hair, the bear didn't make it fifty more yards before it treed again. Rob told me to stay put because he didn't want it to jump out of the tree before the shooter could get there.

We waited for about thirty minutes, all the while enjoying the sound of the dogs at full cry. When the shooter arrived, Rob said he was sending the boy in alone to minimize the noise. He had instructed him to take the shot when he was able to get close enough to see the bear.

The dogs were barking ferociously, and the boy had no trouble sneaking up on the bear. Ten minutes later, we heard a single shot. We ran over and saw he had made a clean shot in the neck, behind the ear. The bear had been killed instantly. The dogs were having a blast chewing on the bear, and this was also great training for the young pups in the pack.

It had been a good kill season so far. We saw several small bears treed and multiple sow bears with cubs. One day, we had dogs running on opposite mountains, and Rob's dogs ended up treeing a sow with cubs. Corey shepherded his dogs down a rather gnarly ridge, very steep and thick with pine and laurel, then up to the first saddle in Wide Hollow. He cut up to the top, then turned right. This led to a part of the mountain that was not hunted much because of the challenging terrain.

Corey hadn't gone two hundred yards across the top of the mountain when he hit a hot track. The dogs ran the bear to the end of the mountain, where it cut down into Stone Coal Gap. It was a steep slope littered with large rocks, small rocks, and shale rocks that made it treacherous to walk up or down—the same slope I had climbed earlier to finish off Barry Lyle's bear. I was sitting just below in my truck, tracking the dogs as they came toward me. Corey only had four dogs on the bear. I was expecting to see the bear at any moment.

But I certainly wasn't expecting what I saw next: a gray fox. I only saw it for a second or two until it scampered into a hole. I was pleased to see the dogs didn't come down the ridge the same way the fox had. Instead, they continued to the right of the fox's path. I stayed where I was, hoping the bear would cross to the other side. If the dogs treed the bear on the opposite side of the road, it would be much easier to get to. Bears were smart, and a lot of the time, they wouldn't cross roads knowing they could get packed on with more dogs. They came to within a hundred yards of the road, paralleled the road for a few hundred yards, then cut left and ran back in the direction they had come from. I watched them go east and up.

I could see on the tracking box that Corey was in the same spot with a young pup that didn't go on the chase. I was watching the dogs get closer and closer to Corey, then cross about twenty yards in front of him. That was when he cut his pup loose to go with the other dogs.

"That bear's a shooter," came Corey's voice over the

radio. The bear ran down into Wide Hollow, then cut down the holler heading north. As it climbed the other side of Wide Hollow, the dogs caught the bear and treed it. Corey, who was still on top of the mountain, told me they sounded good, and that he was going to head down to them.

Another hunter, Austin Salmon, and I hiked up to the dogs, who were less than a mile from us. Wide Hollow was about a mile and a half of gentle slope going up to the saddle. There was a trail that led all the way up, then continued to another road about seven miles away. Despite a few blown-down trees, we made good time along the trail. We were only about two hundred yards away from the dogs when Corey announced he was at the tree.

When we arrived, we found a huge pine tree that was close to three feet in diameter, but no bear. Corey told us to come around to where he was, but we still couldn't see the bear. He told us to look way up. There it was, about seventy feet off the ground, sitting on a large limb.

We climbed a steep bank to get to a better shooting place. We had some other hunters coming to the tree, so we waited for them before Austin took the shot. He was using a rifle, which we were glad about, because it would have been tough to get a precise shot with a pistol, considering the bear's location and height in the tree.

Everyone was now at the tree, so we tied the dogs back and got ready. Oh no! The bear was moving—not down the tree, but up another fifteen feet or so. Austin moved to another spot to get lined up again. From my position, I could still see the bear, but not that well. Austin said he was just waiting for the bear to turn its head in the right direction. He fired the gun, and the bear dropped … onto the limb he was on. The bear was dead, all right, but stuck well over eighty feet off the ground.

"Shoot again," I told Austin, hoping it might make the bear kick a little. He shot again and there was no movement at all. All of us were thinking the same thing: what are we going to do with a dead bear eighty feet up in a tree? Thirty seconds went by as we all looked up, contemplating our next move.

As we watched, the bear's right hind leg gave the slightest jerk, causing the bear to roll off the limb and tumble out of the tree. Two of us took the dogs plus the three pups back down while the others stayed to drag the bear out. We estimated it weighed around 150 pounds.

On the next-to-last day of the season, Rob and I went up for one last hunt. I was coming off a twenty-four–hour shift as a firefighter paramedic, so I wouldn't be home until eight in the morning, and it would be nine before I got to the mountain. Knowing I would be late, Rob said he would try to get a track started prior to my arrival.

When I made it over to the area, Rob was in Stone Coal Gap, and I was on the opposite side of the mountain. I asked Rob on the radio where he needed me. He had four dogs loose, so he asked me to go to the power line parking lot, which was on my side of the mountain, find out where his two dogs were, and keep up with them. He would keep up with the two on his side.

When I arrived at the parking lot, the dogs were three-quarters of a mile above me and tracking west. I paralleled them on the road for four miles as they traveled west, and I could hear them the whole time. For two dogs, they were putting off some good mouth. Then, the bear cut down the mountain and headed back to the east about two miles.

Soon, I could hear the dogs near some large logging equipment. I could tell from the dogs' tone they had caught the bear and were fighting it on the ground. For ten minutes, they sounded great, but then they shut up. Maybe the dogs got whipped a little by the bear, I thought. I wasn't a hundred percent sure why they quit, but they backtracked and crossed over to Rob's side.

"They're on their way to your side now," I told Rob.

"Okay, I'm heading into the woods," he said. "My dogs are showing treed."

I went around the mountain and a mile past Rob's truck. There, in the road, I found the dogs I had been tracking.

I loaded them up and went to find the quickest way into the woods.

"You might as well stay in the truck for now," Rob said. "I'm closing in on them, but it's probably just a cub or a sow with cubs."

I sat there tracking his two bearhounds: Maybell, a Bluetick, and Reno, a Treeing Walker. They seemed to be in the same area, but Reno was about twenty yards below Maybell. Tank was with Rob on his lead about eight hundred yards away, heading west at about the same level on the mountain. I was very concerned now because I wasn't hearing any barking, and there were no bark indicators going off on the tracking collars. Maybell and Reno remained about twenty yards apart, which may have meant two or more bears up two separate trees.

Rob and Tank were now about three hundred yards away with no change in position and no bark indicators. They were showing treed, although that could also mean a dog was just lying down. Okay, now Rob was right on top of the two dogs. Tank's bark indicator was going off at eighty barks per minute. I was very concerned now because Maybell and Reno still had no bark indicators going off. It wasn't unusual for dogs to stop barking for a period of time when they had been at a tree for an extended time. But when a new dog showed up, barking eighty times a minute, and still no bark indicators on Reno and Maybell, I became convinced they had been badly injured or killed.

As these thoughts ran through my mind, Rob shouted over the radio: "I need you up here ASAP! I'm pretty sure Reno is dead, and probably Maybell, too."

"What's going on, Rob?"

"I think the bear killed them and ran. I'm up on a small bluff right now. Tank jumped down and the bear came out and swiped at him and got the tip of his nose, so I pulled Tank up onto the bluff and tied him back. Now I'm getting off this ledge to go kill that bear."

I knew I had a mile-long climb ahead of me. "Okay," I

said. "I'll be there as soon as I can."

The first part of the climb was 250 yards and dizzyingly steep, but then it leveled out on top of a finger ridge and became a gentle-to-moderate slope. I had ventured about four hundred yards from the truck when I heard something. It was Maybell, walking toward me. From a distance, she didn't look well.

As she got closer, I noticed her head had bite marks and she had a puncture wound on the right side of her chest. Her tracking collar was gone. The bear must have ripped it off her. Although she was walking, it was with none of her usual spunk.

I keyed up my radio to tell Rob I had her, but it wouldn't transmit, so I took Maybell back to the truck and used the radio there. "I have Maybell," I said. "Do you want me to take her to the vet?"

"No," his voice came back. "Leave her in the truck and bring me a gun. Get here as quick as you can. I have a bear that wants to kill me and I'm out of bullets!"

I had never felt so anxious about anything before. It terrified me knowing my best friend and hunting partner could be dead before I reached him. I had no communications at all now. My portable radio wasn't working, and I had no cell service. All I could do was hope I got to Rob in time, but I knew it would be at least a thirty-minute climb.

My knees weren't what they used to be and my lungs screamed for air. But I couldn't slow down now. Whenever I could hardly push another foot forward, I'd take a thirty-second break, then press on. Finally, I got to the same elevation as Rob. I was still three hundred yards to his east, but the climb was over, so I was able to catch my breath as I scrambled toward him along the side of the mountain. In the distance, I saw Rob walk a few feet down the hill then stoop down. Relief swept over me. He was alive! I made my way over to him.

"He's breathing," Rob said, glancing up at me as he crouched over Reno's motionless body. "I couldn't get to him until now."

"I didn't think he would make it out alive," I said. "Truthfully, I wasn't sure you would either."

Rob looked up at me and shook his head, then turned his gaze back to the dog on the ground. "We need to get Reno out of here." He pointed down into the holler. "The bear just went down there and lay down. Please go and shoot it."

"No, Rob. That's your bear. You need to finish him for what he did to your dogs."

After he killed the bear, Rob told me he was going to search for Tank, who had pulled his collar off and run away when he heard the shots. He asked me to carry Reno out and take him to the vet—if he was still alive.

Rob had already called his daughter Ashley, a veterinarian assistant, and told her what had happened to Maybell. The second she got his call, she told everyone in the vet office that Maybell had been badly injured. She rushed over, got Maybell out of the truck, and brought her back to the vet.

Reno remained motionless, but still breathing, as I carried him out. I hiked straight down the holler, taking short breaks to check on him from time to time. It was the longer route, but considering I was carrying a seventy-pound dog, I knew it would be easier than the way I had come in.

To my great relief, Reno was still breathing when I got down to Stone Coal Gap Road, and I upped his probability of survival from zero to five percent. It was still half a mile to my truck, so I left Reno lying beside the road. After carrying all that weight a mile and a half down the holler, I made good time on the gentle incline of the gravel road.

I hollered at Rob from the truck radio. "I'm in the truck now, heading back to get Reno."

"10-4," he replied. "Tank and I are with Reno now. He's still breathing, thank God."

"I'll be there in a minute." I floored it and drove like the wind, basically dirt tracking it over to Reno. You'd almost think I'd been driving an ambulance my whole life. We put

Reno up front with me while Rob and Tank rode on the tailgate back to his truck, where I slowed just enough to let them jump down. Then I sped off to the vet as fast as I could, leaving tire marks as I slid around curves.

I was making excellent time on the hardtop road, glancing occasionally at Reno to make sure he was still breathing. Then I pulled up behind a vehicle that was just creeping along. Well, maybe going the speed limit, but in my haste, it seemed much slower. I couldn't pass. I was stuck.

"Come on, come on!" I pleaded.

Fortunately, the vehicle turned off the road after another half mile, and I hammered the gas. I veered onto the main road, and Reno made the first move I had seen him make yet: he pushed himself onto the floor with his hind feet. As I swung into the vet's parking lot, practically on two wheels, Ashley came running outside.

"Where's Reno?"

"He's on the front floorboard." She scooped him up and ran inside. I followed her in, but I was so physically and mentally exhausted that I had a hard time even walking the short distance to the surgical table. I stood there watching. After a few minutes, the vet looked up at me and shook his head.

"I'm so sorry," he said. "Reno is brain dead. He's not going to make it."

I was heartbroken. Ashley took me back to see Maybell, who was standing and wagging her tail. She looked better, but she was still going to require more surgeries for her chest wound. Even so, it was wonderful to see her and know she would be okay. I was relieved that one dog had made it, but I was still sad about Reno.

I called Rob and delivered the news. He told me his son Tyler had left work early to come help with the bear. Tyler worked for Rob in an automotive garage, so he was able to leave the second he got Rob's frantic call about the bear that was trying to kill him. Rob asked me to come back to Stone Coal Gap.

When I pulled up, I rolled down my window. Rob said Tyler was with the bear and just about to drag it out as far as he could, and that a few more people were on their way to help Tyler with the drag. He climbed into my truck and plopped down on the passenger seat. We were both drained. It was hard to know how stressful a situation like this could be until living through it.

For the first time, we were able to talk face to face about everything that had happened. Rob told me that even though Tank was going crazy, he didn't think the bear was still around. As it turned out, the bear was back up in a ravine and he just couldn't see it. That was when Tank jumped down and the bear appeared out of nowhere and swiped his nose.

Even though he could see Reno wasn't moving, Rob knew he had to take care of the bear before he could do anything for Reno. "I knew Reno was dead," he said. "I also knew from the tracking box that Maybell was there in the ravine with the bear, which meant she was probably dead, too."

After tying Tank back, Rob had eased down the ravine to get a shot off at the bear. He wasn't able to physically get to a location where he could see the bear because he knew it would charge him like it had just charged Tank. So he pointed his gun in the direction he thought the bear was in, and pulled the trigger. The bear let out a squall. Rob racked another .45-70 shell into his rifle and shot again. This time, the bear charged him.

"I was able to get another shot off as he was charging," Rob said. "I was about to reload and shoot again when I realized my gun was empty." The shot had slowed the bear down, but the bear was still coming at him. He ran out of the ravine and reached into his pocket for more shells. That was when he realized he had left all his extra shells in the truck. Quickly, Rob ducked behind a tree that was about three feet in diameter and tried to keep out of sight while the bear played a game of "Ring Around the Rosie" with him.

When the bear finally lay down in the ravine, Rob found Maybell's collar and left it strapped to the bear so Tyler could track to it later. Then he walked down to where Reno was to pay his last respects, which was where I had found him.

"I was totally surprised to see he was still alive," Rob said. "I think he had probably been lying there for at least an hour, if not longer. I was thinking it was a miracle Reno was still breathing, and it was even more of a miracle that he was still alive when you got him to the vet."

It was terrifying to think about how determined this bear had been to kill Rob. Normally, when a bear charged, it was simply trying to escape a dangerous situation. But this bear was genuinely looking to kill someone, and that someone was Rob. Thank God he had managed to slow the bear down enough to stay away from it.

As we talked, Cody Morris and one other hunter showed up. Soon after, Tyler came walking down the road and told us he had dragged the bear down the holler, and had it most of the way out, but would need help hauling it up and over the ridge. Tyler, Cody, and the other hunter climbed the ridge, dropped down to get the bear, and had it back at the truck forty-five minutes later.

We got an update on Maybell: her surgery was finished, and she was doing very well. The vet said if there was no change in Maybell's condition, Rob could come and pick her up later that evening. That night, Maybell went home and enjoyed a luxury stay at the hunt club. She was still sore and walking slowly, but she would live to hunt another bear.

That same evening, Rob told me Reno was now conscious, despite sustaining a closed head injury from the force of the bear's slap and being declared brain dead. Rob said he would know more by morning.

He called me the next morning and told me Reno had taken a turn for the better. He was now standing, although he was still weak, and the vet thought he might be blind in one eye. But that evening, Reno was able to come home and join Maybell. I came by to help cut up the bear, and it was great seeing the dogs together again. Those two were practically joined at the hip while hunting. When we took them outside to do their business, I could tell they were very sore, judging by how gingerly they were walking.

At her next vet appointment, Maybell had her drainage tubes removed. By now, she was acting more herself. Not a hundred percent yet, but clearly in much less pain. Reno hadn't lost his eyesight after all and was healing well from his head injury. Days ago, I didn't think Reno would even make it off the mountain alive, and now it looked like both he and Maybell would be hunting again later that year.

On the first day of chase season, we took the dogs up to Stone Coal Gap and hunted to the left of the road. We sent the dogs up the trail, and when they reached the top of the mountain, they got a strike. They split up, with Reno and Maybell heading off to the east by themselves while the rest of the dogs cut west. Both packs appeared to be running hot tracks.

Reno and Maybell dropped down the other side of the mountain toward the dump and got halfway down before they headed back west and climbed slightly. Minutes later, they had treed the bear near the power line, 0.7 miles from the parking lot.

Cody Morris hiked up there and reported that the bear was in a small tree, about a foot in diameter. Since it was likely the bear would jump out of such a small tree if he approached, Cody said he would wait for us to get there before moving closer. We arrived fifteen minutes later to find the bear still there, less than ten feet off the ground. Reno and Maybell were at the base, hammering the tree.

That was one of my best trees yet. These were two dogs we thought we had lost back in January. Leading a seriously injured Maybell back to the truck and carrying Reno's near-lifeless body off the mountain was so mentally and physically draining that just seeing these two back in the game, doing what they loved, did my heart a lot of good. I could not have asked for a better opening day of chase season.

CHAPTER 15
My Grandson Landon

In the first chapter, I told you a little bit about my granddad. But now I'd like to introduce you to Landon Levi Gutshall, my grandson. I've been calling him my grandson, but he is actually my great grandson. Judy and I have had custody of Landon since he was three years old, and he is the sweetest child I've ever known.

We noticed at a young age he wasn't quite like other kids. After some testing from a couple of pediatricians, he was diagnosed with autism. However, he is very smart and is considered high-functioning autistic.

As a toddler, his vocabulary consisted of three or four words, and it was difficult to understand him, so we took him to speech therapy twice a week for more than three years. Today, you wouldn't know he ever had any speech issues. He loves to talk, but if he's around someone he doesn't know, we still have to pull words out of him. Sometimes this even happens when he's around family and friends, but not as much.

We signed him up for Cub Scouts once he was old enough to join. I was an Eagle Scout and loved my time in the Scouts. Landon rose quickly through the ranks, from Lion to Arrow of Light. Scouting was a great outlet for Landon. He had always had a hard time socializing with other kids his age, but the Cub Scouts helped him come out of his cocoon and make friends with his fellow Scouts. It also helped pry him away from his computer games for a little while. He still enjoys our many adventures and is always looking forward to the next meeting or outing.

When he was nine years old, he was showing traits of a true outdoorsman, so I introduced him to shooting sports.

I would have done it sooner, but with his autism, I didn't feel he was ready until then. I had shot my first gun, a .22 caliber rifle, at the age of three (although that was nothing compared to Daniel Boone, who had not only shot a gun, but had *killed a bear* at the age of three. Can you tell Daniel Boone is my hero?).

With Landon, it was a little slow going, as he was afraid of guns and thought they might hurt him. But I was patient with him, and Santa Claus even brought him a .410 shotgun for Christmas, which we always kept locked in a safe and took out only under my supervision. It was a gun he could use for squirrel hunting as well as deer hunting. But he was having a hard time with the open sights, and we didn't have much luck that year.

The following year, I added a scope to my .30 carbine rifle, which greatly improved Landon's accuracy. I took him deer hunting, and when he went to shoot his very first deer, he got a sudden case of buck fever and missed. But then a spike buck happened along. Landon took careful aim, pulled the trigger, and hit the deer. It ran about twenty yards before it fell. We walked over and discovered he had shot a unicorn, meaning a deer with only one antler. The other antler had broken close to the skull and was bright white: a fresh break. Landon was very happy getting his first deer.

When Landon entered the Boy Scouts, he excelled there, too. I became an Assistant Scoutmaster so I could accompany him on his outdoor adventures. To this day, I love being with the troop and watching the Scouts grow and mature along the path to Eagle Scout.

Landon's first camping trip was to Caldwell Fields when he was ten years old. I couldn't attend because I had to work, so this would be his first time away from Judy and me. I was a little apprehensive, but I knew that the Scoutmaster and Assistant Scoutmasters, along with all the older Scouts, would make this a fun and enjoyable adventure for him.

My wife, on the other hand, was very nervous about it. If I couldn't go, she said, Landon shouldn't either. I told her not to worry. He would be taken care of, and the confidence he gained would be invaluable. So Landon went on his own, and when he got back, he couldn't stop talking about what a great time he'd had.

He also went camping with the Boy Scouts at Devil's Marbleyard. This was a mountainside full of gigantic boulders to hike across. Everyone had an awesome time. He also went on a two-night camping trip to the James River, and we got to paddle a canoe down the river for ten miles. Landon also attended the Klondike Derby, an event where Scout troops take their sleds to different areas to compete against other troops.

The Derby was in February, and the overnight temperature dropped to around twenty degrees on the night they arrived. The following day, the high temperature barely made it out of the thirties, with wind strong enough to break two of the three 10 x 10–foot canopies they had set up.

We also had an overnighter where all the Scouts worked on their Horsemanship merit badges. It was Landon's first time going horseback riding. He was able to complete all but a couple of requirements for the badge and will be finishing them later this year.

We also have two more camping trips planned this year: the first is to Smith Mountain Lake, which will have waterskiing, a new adventure for Landon. The second is a canoeing trip at Philpott Lake, which has an island we can camp on. During that trip, Landon will be camp cook and will achieve the rank of First Class.

Landon is having a blast in the Scouts, as is his Paw Paw. Getting him off his computer is an ongoing challenge, but he's all in for anything Scouts related.

When Landon was eleven years old, we caught the opening day of youth deer hunting season. We crawled out of bed well before daylight (which Landon is not a fan of, unless it's for hunting or something Scouts related, in which case all I have to do is softly say, "Hey, Landon, the deer are waiting on us," and he's out of that bed, bushy-tailed, and ready to hunt).

In the silence of pre-dawn, we climbed into the truck. The air was heavy and still, with fog so thick you could cut it with a knife. We drove five miles to the field we were hunting and set our chairs out. I had brought a lightweight sawhorse for him to use as a shooting platform. Landon had a new rifle, a Ruger .300 Blackout. He had practiced with it quite a bit and was shooting very well.

It was still dark when we finished setting up. I scanned the field in front of me and to my left while Landon scanned to his right. Shortly after daybreak, Landon whispered, "Paw Paw, I see one!"

I turned. To my right, shrouded in fog, was the silhouette of a deer. I couldn't make out any antlers, but it was either-sex hunting for youth days, so it didn't matter. The deer was looking off to its left, not moving. There was a knoll in front of us, and my concern was that by the time Landon got down on the shooting platform, he wouldn't be able to see the deer. I told Landon if we gave it a little time, the deer would probably wander in our direction and give us a better shot. But for five minutes, the deer didn't move.

"I can see it just fine," Landon said. "I can shoot it."

I estimated the deer to be over a hundred yards away. "If you have a good shot, take your time and aim carefully," I told him.

When he fired, the deer took off running. "Paw Paw, I missed him."

"No, you didn't," I said. "You hit him hard."

I knew it was a good shot because as the deer ran, he was practically on his front knees, pushing himself forward with his hind legs. He ran twenty yards, then went down.

"Paw Paw, it's a buck!" Landon exclaimed as we walked down toward the deer.

I got excited when he said that. All I could see through the dense fog was the outline of a deer, and I thought it was a doe. But as we got closer, I made out antlers. It turned out to be a nine-point buck with a fifteen-inch spread. All the target practice I did with Landon had paid off: it was a perfect lung and heart shot. Not bad for his second deer. When I paced it off to measure the distance, it was 110 yards.

That Monday was the start of the three-day early bear season. I had taken the day off work, and I allowed Landon to skip school to go hunting with me. Since the next day was my scheduled day off, I was planning to let Landon miss that day, too, but only if he wasn't successful today. I didn't tell him that, though, because if he did kill a bear today, I didn't want him to miss another day of school.

We got an early start and drove thirty minutes to the mountain. There, we met up with half the group, led by Daniel Perdue. The other half would be coming up from the other side of the mountain. Landon and I stayed on the road to track the dogs as two or three people led each pack of dogs up opposite sides of the mountain. I could only track the ones on my side of the mountain, at least until the other dogs got higher up.

It wasn't long before the dogs I was following hit a cold track. They tried to heat it up, but the track was too cold, so the dogs were placed back on their leads, and they continued up the mountain. After another half mile, they hit a cold track again, but this time the dogs managed to stay with it, albeit slowly.

By the time the dogs were halfway up the mountain, I was able to track the dogs that had come up from the other side. The bear was about half a mile in front of our pack. At this point, the two packs weren't even close together—ours was well below and to the east of the pack on top—but it looked like our dogs had actually pushed the bear to the other pack.

Soon, all the dogs joined forces and ran the bear off the mountain, right toward me and Landon. It looked like the bear was going to cross the road close to where we were sitting, so we drove down the road hoping we could turn the bear.

The dogs were now 150 yards from us in the roadway. The sound of my truck had caused the bear to turn around, exactly as I intended. All the land on the other side of the road was private, so not only would it have ended the hunt had they crossed, but we also would have had to go in—without guns—

to get the dogs.

Instead, the dogs and bear ran back up to within a hundred yards of the top of the mountain and treed there. The sound of fifteen dogs at full cry was music to my ears. Landon and I were now looking for the best route for the mile-long hike up the mountain. This was Landon's bear, so those who were already up there were holding the tree for us.

We started the steep climb up the mountain and bore to our left. The dogs at the tree were at full cry and easy to hear, so we didn't need the tracking box at all. They sounded even better when we arrived at the tree forty-five minutes later. The bear had run up a tree that was almost three feet in diameter and was now standing on a limb that was over a foot in diameter. He was twenty-five feet off the ground, up against the trunk of the tree with all four feet close together on the branch. This early in the season, the trees were in full foliage, making it harder to see the bear through the leaves, but I estimated it to be between 275 and 300 pounds.

Before taking the bear, Landon waited for a few more hunters to arrive from the other side of the mountain. While we waited, I found a good spot for him to shoot from, then had him look at the bear through the scope of his rifle to let his nerves wear off.

"Paw Paw, that's a big bear."

I nodded. "Just take your time and get a good shot off. Everyone should be here soon. I'll let you know when to shoot."

When all hunters were present, Landon took aim at the bear's neck, just behind the ear, and pulled the trigger. The bear just flinched a little, so Landon took a few more shots at the chest cavity, and it fell out of the tree dead.

Once the bear was on the ground, I got my first look at it. Bears tended to put on a lot of weight prior to denning up, but this one hadn't put on very much. Even so, it was very long and had a large belly, so I revised my initial estimate to four hundred pounds, or thereabouts.

Of the ten people on top of the mountain, half took the

hounds down while the other half of us started down with the bear. Most of the drag down the mountain consisted of gently tugging on the dog leads we had tied around the bear as it rolled downhill on its own. That was, until it ran into a tree, at which point two or three of us would tug at the leads and get it going again.

Once we were lower on the mountain, we actually had to drag it, but three of us were able to handle it without issue. We had to attach a few more dog leads once the mountain flattened out, but at this point, all of us were dragging the bear.

It felt good to reach the road, where we only had a short hike to my truck. It took all five of us to load the bear onto my dog box. The entire dog box was covered, with part of the bear even hanging off the end. Largest bear I ever had on my dog box.

I drove to my next-door neighbor's house to skin the bear and place it in his cooler. When we weighed the animal, it tipped the scale at 380 pounds. My on-ground guesstimate was close, although my initial, in-tree guess was off by over a hundred pounds.

I took a close look at the bear's neck. Landon had placed his first shot perfectly, which surprised me, given it had only caused the bear to jump a little. But it was clear that the .300 Blackout just wasn't enough gun for going through that much bone to get to the spinal cord. I can't express how proud I was of Landon. On his first hunting trip three years ago, he was having a hard time traversing the mountains, but now he had no trouble at all.

Landon is now twelve years old and has achieved the rank of Second Class in the Boy Scouts. He's attending his second week-long summer camp at Camp Raven Knob, which is where I am writing this. I couldn't make it to his first summer camp at Camp Powhatan, but he had a great time there and earned many of his requirements. He now has six merit badges, and upon leaving Camp Raven Knob, he will have completed, or nearly completed, six more.

One of these is the Swimming merit badge, which requires a swim test. Landon will have to jump into water that's over his head, swim seventy-five yards with any approved stroke, then twenty-five yards of backstroke, then float for one minute without touching anything. Last year, Landon was disappointed to have been classified as "beginner" and not "swimmer" after his test. I wanted to make sure he was ready for the next test, so this past spring I got him a membership and swim lessons at the YMCA, and he passed his test with flying colors. I feel so blessed to be here at Camp Raven Knob, enjoying nature. I can't think of a better setting for writing this last chapter.

We have come full circle from my rough, tough, burly granddad whose stories made me a lifelong bear hunter. I'm so fortunate to have been able to hear those tales. Here's a suggestion for you young folks out there: sit down with a journal every night and record your day. You never know when the urge to write a book may hit you. I never thought I would write a book, but here I am. Had I kept a journal of my granddad's stories, I could have written an entire book with just those stories alone.

It was Rob Cook who made bear hunting a possibility for me, and it has consumed my life since the nineties. And it was my wife, Judy, who put up with me being gone most of the month of December every year, from well before daylight to well after dark on many nights, and on as many weekends as I could during chase season.

The best part of this whole story is that the tradition will live on. I have turned my adventurous grandson into a bear hunter. Landon is so precious to me, and spending time with him in the great outdoors has been an awesome experience, whether it's camping, fishing, canoeing, a Scouting event, or my passion in life, bear hunting. Landon is my real-life, modern-day Daniel Boone, my hero.

Bonus Section

Dale's World-Famous Bear Ribs

Over the years, I've learned several different ways to cook bear. The process always starts the same way: boiling the meat three separate times and pouring off the water between boils. I like to remove as much of the fat as I can before doing this.

After boiling, one way to prepare the meat is to put it in an oven bag and roast it in the oven. It only takes an additional hour since the meat is mostly cooked already. Sometimes I'll add onions, carrots, potatoes, celery, and garlic to the bag as it cooks. It's delicious.

Another method is to cut the meat into chunks and put those in a crock-pot with cream of mushroom soup. You can add veggies to this if you like, but it's delicious either way.

You can also just boil the meat a little more and throw veggies in for the last boiling.

But now let's talk about the best way to prepare bear meat, because you haven't had ribs until you've had my bear ribs. As before, I start by boiling the ribs and pouring off the water three times. Again, I remove as much fat as I can before boiling. This involves separating the layers slightly to remove some of the fat between layers.

My favorite way to finish it once it comes out of the boiling water is to place it in an offset smoker with a dry rub. You can experiment to see what your favorite rub is, but I have tried several different rubs and most have turned out very well. I usually smoke it at low temperature, about 225 degrees, for three hours. I remove it, baste it in barbecue sauce, then place it in foil and throw it back into the smoker for another 30–45 minutes.

This process can also be done in the oven by baking it on low heat, using the dry rub first and then the barbecue sauce. It works, but using the smoker makes for better-tasting ribs. I've eaten a lot of ribs in my life, but my own bear ribs are the best I've ever had. Maybe I need to open a restaurant chain called Dale's World-Famous Bear Ribs.

I didn't plan on turning this memoir into a cookbook, but consider it a bonus for reading my book. I hope this book inspires you to give bear hunting a try. If nothing else, your reward will be fresh, delicious bear meat.

About the Author

Dale Thacker is a seasoned bear hunter, firefighter paramedic, and avid outdoorsman from Troutville, Virginia. He and his wife, Judy, have been married over forty years and live with their many pets, including the love of their lives, a black teacup poodle named CoCo. Dale's twelve-year-old grandson, Landon, is in the Boy Scouts and becoming a bear hunter himself. In addition to hunting, Dale also loves fishing, camping, hiking, and enjoying the great outdoors. *Tales of a Bear Hunter* is Dale's debut work.

More from Dale Thacker

Look for *Marijuana Bear*, coming soon.

www.ingramcontent.com/pod-product-compliance
Lightning Source LLC
LaVergne TN
LVHW041219080426
835508LV00011B/1002